Journey to the Fourth

KU-799-285

The Kali Gandaki is one of the world's most violent
rivers. To the people of Nepal it is the Goddess of
Death, yet another hazard in a country burdened
with disease and infant mortality. But to the
country's pioneering Christian medical missionaries
it has always been seen as a potential agent for life —
a possible highway through the mountains, linking
homes with hospitals.

Taking specially-designed new hovercraft, a 26-man
British Joint Services Expedition set out to try to
harness this previously unnavigable river. *Journey to
the Fourth World* is the leader's account of this
adventurous and testing expedition and its results in
and beyond Nepal. It is also the account of his
determination to use all means possible to help
Christian relief work in the world's poorest countries
— the Fourth World.

JOURNEY TO THE FOURTH WORLD

by Michael Cole

A LION PAPERBACK

Published by
Lion Publishing
Icknield Way, Tring, Herts, England
ISBN 0 85648 361 3 (paperback)
ISBN 0 85648 410 5 (cased)
Albatross Books
PO Box 320, Sutherland, NSW 2232, Australia
ISBN 0 86760 290 2 (paperback)
ISBN 0 86760 325 9 (cased)

This edition 1981

The photographs in this book are reproduced by
kind permission of:
Baptist Missionary Society, page 11
Ed Chase, pages 89, 187
Mike Cole, pages 24, 37, 45, 97, 105, 113, 121, 129,
    139, 155
Bernard Coleman, pages 29, 53, 171
Brian Goodwin, pages 59, 81
Mick Reynolds, page 67

Printed and bound by Richard Clay
(The Chaucer Press) Ltd, Bungay, Suffolk

Contents

Foreword by Sir Neil Cameron

Foreword

It was my honour to be patron of the Joint Services River Rover Expedition to the great and dangerous Kali Gandaki river of Nepal. It was a team effort in every sense, but it was clear from the early briefings that the team was going to be led superbly by Mike Cole, a Royal Air Force officer with considerable experience and motivated by a strong Christian faith. It was this faith which enabled him to keep the expedition going when faced with a wide variety of obstacles — not least the bureaucracy common to many countries.

I believe that the Kali Gandaki expedition will prove to be of historic importance, particularly in harnessing simple and easily-maintained technology to ease the suffering and hardship of those living on the edge of survival in the difficult parts of the world. There are hopeful signs that the decade we have just entered will see a quickening interest in the plight of many in the Third World and the Fourth World (to use the author's expression). I hope those who are concerned with this work will read this book and take note of its lesson.

Finally, as a Christian, my admiration goes out to missionaries working in such conditions as those the expedition encountered in Nepal. They deserve all our help, encouragement and prayers.

Both the expedition and the book have given me considerable spiritual encouragement and I am sure this will be the case for all who read it. It is a splendid book — well written and gripping.

Marshal of the Royal Air Force Sir Neil Cameron
GCB, CBE, DSO, DFC, AE
Former Chief of the Defence Staff
Principal, King's College, London

Mike Cole, the Christian adventurer, with a Nepali Hindu priest.

ONE

THE CHALLENGE

Walking down the trail, I looked up to where the sky should be — and there was a mountain instead. This was Nepal! My breath was caught by the exceptional beauty and sheer variety of the jagged peaks of the Himalayan backdrop.

Looking down, across the villages dotted on the hillside, my eyes went to a very different picture. The warm and friendly people are subject to so much suffering and premature death. For the sick and injured in the remote villages of west Nepal the dilemma is desperate.

In one village, a moment's inattention has caused the eldest son of a Nepali family to plunge down from a tall tree while cutting leaves for the goats. The bones in his leg are shattered. The terrain is so tortuous that the father will have to carry his son on his back for eight days to get medical aid from the mission hospital at Tansen. This will take him away from the fields. If he doesn't plant the rice, the whole family may die. If he doesn't get help for his son, only one person will die — probably from gangrenous infection — or, at best, be crippled for the rest of his life.

They decide to take the boy and risk the rice-planting. From their village, perched precariously on the mountainside, surrounded by the carefully-terraced fields awaiting the rice seed, they set off at dawn. It has been an awful night. No one could sleep as the boy moaned, groaned and sweated through the interminable hours of darkness. They contrive to make a kind of sitting stretcher out of a *doko*, the large wicker basket normally used for carrying the produce of the fields. The father hoists this onto his back, bending forwards and taking the strain on his forehead with the *namlo*, the canvas band.

The boy, pale and with beads of perspiration on his upper lip, grits his teeth as they wave farewell to his mother, younger brothers and sisters. So they begin the long, arduous trek down and along the twisting, narrow stony track. The sun rises higher in the sky and glints on the Kali Gandaki, illuminating it like a silver ribbon threading its way through the valley.

Like many of Nepal's mighty rivers, the Kali Gandaki, which the Nepalis call the 'Goddess of Death', is a natural but formidable highway. As it makes its way south through the Himalayan range, between the steep sides of the deepest river gorge in the world, its path is strewn with turbulent rapids. At intervals it is traversed by swaying footbridges which mark the crossing-points of the well-trodden paths which for centuries have been the highways of Nepal.

If only a craft could be found which could operate safely on the Kali Gandaki, the father's days of travelling from his remote village to the nearest medical help could be shrunk to a few hours . . .

18 December 1978 was a fine clear day as River Rover 01 took to the fast-flowing Kali Gandaki. For the twenty-six members of the expedition, it was the moment of truth. The project which had brought together a team of men from many varied back-

Nepal's ambulance service is non-existent. The sick
have to be carried for days in an improvised
stretcher or harness.

grounds to a bridge on this river in west Nepal, was the result of two strands stretching back several years.

One day during the miners' strike in the winter of 1973, I was sitting in my office at Royal Air Force Bentley Priory, waiting for the lights to go out from another power cut, when I was visited by Patrick Goodland, local pastor of Stanmore Baptist Church and part-time RAF chaplain. Pat placed a photograph on my desk. It showed a group of emaciated children's bodies lying in the back of a Land Rover.

Pat unfolded the story, little-known at the time, of the victims of the famine in the Wollo province of Ethiopia. Thousands were dying for lack of water. I was disturbed by what I saw — and sat up when it dawned on me that Pat actually wanted me to do something about it. Surely this was a job for the Red Cross or the United Nations, or some such agency with real resources? But a Christian relief organization called TEAR Fund had a sixteen-ton water-drilling rig in Britain, and Pat was now asking my help and that of Squadron Leader Dick Bell to get it to Ethiopia.

It was as simple and as complicated as that.

Air marshals control major airlift movements, not squadron leaders. There was a national shortage of aircraft fuel and the country was in the grip of a three-day working week. Should I tangle my commitment to the local church with my secular job? These were the issues. But Pat Goodland was not easily put off.

So developed a project with a real purpose. A small six-man team undertook to shift this massive piece of equipment 3,000 miles to East Africa. No RAF aircraft could be made available for several weeks, but we found a civilian Hercules which normally moved oil pipelines for BP in Alaska. Unusually heavy frost had frozen the pipes, and the Hercules was available for us to use.

After overcoming technical problems and endless battles with bureaucracy, plus the dust and rubble of the road to Wollo, we delivered the rig to the famine area. Our reward was the transparent joy in the faces of the suffering Ethiopian people and their gratitude for the simple aid. The engineers in our team used the rig to bring fresh life-giving water to the parched surface. Many thousands of lives were saved as a result of the seventy wells that were sunk in the months following.

For me the result of this experience was far-reaching. In Ethiopia, Pat Goodland contracted typhus. But his reaction was to compare the sophisticated treatment he received in a London hospital with the pitifully inadequate health care we had witnessed among the Ethiopian victims of the disease. His selfless determination showed me that the efforts of one dedicated man could still make a real difference.

Since my days as a boy scout, and later during my Service career as an RAF Physical Education Officer, I had taken part in numerous expeditions in the spirit of climbing the hill 'because it was there'. Now I had seen a new type of expedition. The terrain and deprivations of Ethiopia provided all the ingredients necessary for a challenging adventure but, at the same time, responding to the challenge had a fulfilled a useful purpose.

Java, Hong Kong, Cyprus. I became involved in a succession of leave-time activities over the next few years, all of which underlined the usefulness of such humanitarian expeditions. In February 1975 an X-ray unit was needed by a Salvation Army hospital at Turen in Java. I planned to combine the delivery of this with a trek up the volcanic Mount Bromo.

'Salvation Army men still believe in miracles,' read the signal from the British Embassy, Jakarta. This was not meant to quicken our faith in God's providence, but to quash our expectations of swiftly moving half a ton of X-ray equipment through the intricacies of Indonesian customs. Working within a tight leave schedule I had anticipated problems. Instead the three members of our project team were hard pressed to keep up with their X-ray equipment! After 9,000 miles it arrived just one hour before we reached the hospital.

In Hong Kong, the Chinese Discovery Sailing Centre needed Mirror dinghies. Our reward for supplying them was to experience junk sailing in a turbulent sea.

On 17 January 1975 my settled life in our comfortable Stanmore home was again disturbed, this time by the arrival of a letter from Dr Bill Gould, the medical director at Tansen mission hospital in west Nepal.

'. . . The project I have in mind envisages using a hovercraft on one of Nepal's main rivers, the Kali Gandaki. The river in part makes the northern border of the Palpa district which I liken to a large English county. However, this county-sized area has only one road. The river therefore has the potential for transportation backwards and forwards as we carry out health care. Three or four days' journey could be reduced to a mere few hours. My hope is that starting from the base we could set up four health posts along our stretch of the river and serve a population of 20,000 people. Our brief from government is that we should open six health posts over the next five years. This has tremendous potential.

'Therefore, Mike, I am asking you personally to explore the possibility of bringing a suitable hovercraft to Nepal. I do hope you will be able to help us.'

I had received another unmistakable challenge!

I knew that experiments had been made in the use of lightweight hovercraft. It might be possible to find a suitable craft. I shared this challenge with burly RAF sergeant, Bob Abbott.

A minor problem at the Tansen hospital was the lack of an internal telephone system. Frequently at night the whole medical staff would be called out for an emergency when just one particular member of the staff was required. Bob and I undertook to deliver the exchange equipment to Tansen and at the same time to 'recce' the River Kali Gandaki.

News of our intended visit spread quickly amongst the friends of missionaries serving in Nepal. Parcels arrived from far and wide for us to take. Thai International Airways were very accommodating, as our hand baggage clocked in at over 200 pounds.

Bob is one of the strongest men I have ever known, so this baggage was never evenly distributed. More important was Bob's strength of character as we tackled the necessary hurdles to get ourselves and our telephone exchange to Tansen. Strangers in Nepal have always had to get permission to act in a new way, and this applies just as much today as it did to the first European visitors to Nepal, the Capuchin monks, 250 years ago.

After a half-hour journey, we arrived at the United Mission guest house at Thapathali in Kathmandu. We unloaded the parcels into the courtyard from the battered, bulging taxi we had taken from the airport and introduced ourselves. News of our intended visit had not filtered through and although our service haircuts made it clear that we were not hippies, we might easily have been 'world travellers' . . . A bed for the night was offered in the outhouse!

Returning to the courtyard we delivered our substantial hand baggage. The eyes of the hostess of the guest house widened visibly. 'Friend, come up higher' was the clear message as Bob and I were shown to the special guest room. Simple gifts from home such as favourite spreads, toilet soap, last week's women's magazines and yesterday's daily paper are very welcome to these front-line Christian workers who are cut off from such everyday Western items.

At supper we met Dr Carl Fredericks, one of the pioneers who entered Nepal in 1951 when, soon after the end of the Rana era, the country cautiously opened her doors to the outside world. A visionary, Carl had early seen the communication potential of the rivers. Ten years previously he had travelled down part of the Kali Gandaki on a large inflated tyre, but even on a warm day his chilled limbs had prevented more than a few miles' progress.

The Fredericks had started their missionary service in south China but had been evacuated when the Communists took over. On their medical tour to west Nepal in 1951-52, Carl and Betty had taken with them their three children, the youngest barely two months old. They planned to visit Tansen and conduct a clinic. They quickly made friends in the town and in their first six weeks treated 1,500 patients. Carl was asked to perform an operation with 200 spectators watching through the door and windows of the room. When he displayed the large bladder stone he had removed, a spontaneous cheer rose from the onlookers. The governor urged them to consider opening a permanent hospital. And so Tansen Hospital was born.

When we outlined our ideas for bringing a hovercraft to the Kali Gandaki, Dr Fredericks expressed his enthusiasm for the project.

Next morning we took a twenty-minute flight by an AVRO 748 aircraft from Kathmandu to Pokhara, thus saving a day's journey on the mountain road. North of Pokhara the splendour and size of the Machhapuchhare and the Annapurna ranges gave us the finest mountain view we had ever seen. We took a bus south from Pokhara to Tansen on a road of over 1,000 bends. Frequent stops were made to top up the radiator as the bus negotiated the tortuous route. The devastating results of the landslides which occur along this route during the monsoon season were apparent every few miles.

Tansen is 200 miles west of Kathmandu. The bazaar is a mecca for traders following the time-worn route from Tibet to India. Smells ranged from the pungent

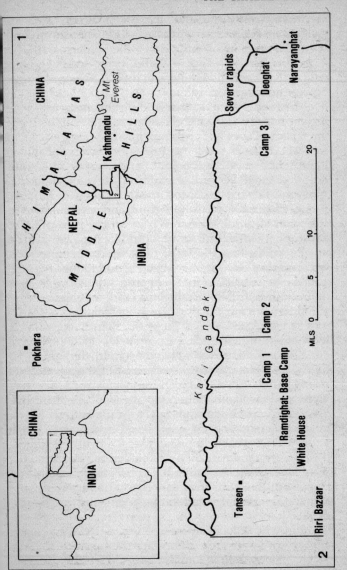

spices used to flavour the staple diet of rice to misused
toilet areas — anywhere public and anywhere convenient seemed to be usual.

At the hospital, Dr Bill Gould introduced us to his
colleagues from Sweden, Australia, Norway, USA,
Canada and UK. Australian nurse Gwen Coventry, the
health worker in charge of the distant dispensary at
Buling near the Kali Gandaki, discussed with us how
we were to carry out our assignment.

The river's only vehicle bridging-point at
Ramdighat was to be our starting-point. From
Ramdighat we set out to explore the river along its
west-east flow, parallel to the Mahabharat mountain
range. Our task was to photograph and note the river's
characteristics in order to report on the type of flow
and rapids that a hovercraft would have to negotiate.

We found that the swift flow was punctuated by
bends as the river met hard rock bends. Crumbly rock
areas were subject to frequent landslides. A rock face
on one bank usually produced a sandbank opposite —
an ideal site for landing the hovercraft. We made
quicker progress across these sandbanks, keeping a
look-out for quicksands. On one such beach I trod on a
large snakeskin, fortunately deserted by the snake. At
night, we slept under the verandas of the typical two-
storey huts, timber-framed with straw finish. We
were made welcome wherever we went, even in this
area where few Europeans apart from health workers
ever venture to go.

In west Nepal the monsoon season continues from
June to September. This was November, and as the
water-level fell, the difficulty of the rapids would increase until the next year's monsoon flooded the river
again. We carefully noted the high and low water
marks. It seemed likely that any hovercraft operations
would be limited to a nine-month period from September until mid-June each year.

Our trek ended at Rani, where, close to the river, a

former ruling Rana had built a palace as a memorial to one of his queens. From the decaying splendour of a former age we trekked back to Tansen to discuss our findings with Bill Gould. His needs were simple. The thinly-spread team of medical workers of the Palpa district of west Nepal spent a large proportion of their time on weary treks. The Kali Gandaki provided a natural, difficult, but potentially usable, highway. The successful delivery and trials of a suitable lightweight hovercraft which could perform as a 'Land Rover of the river' could do much to bring a better quality of life to the people of this remote mountain area.

Ke garne, 'What to do?', is a favourite Nepali phrase when a hurdle lies ahead. What to do, indeed? The challenge had been reinforced.

TWO

THE EXPEDITION IS BORN

The difficulties facing Nepal are not unique. In the least developed countries of the world there are enormous problems of population increase, of poor crops and of people permanently malnourished and living on the brink of ill health and so functioning at half pace. For the sick, the suffering is desperate, yet this is only the tip of the iceberg.

There are two schools of thought as to how the affluent should react to the so-called 'Fourth World'. Some think that the West should rationalize its wealth and apply 'lifeboat ethics': each rich country will survive only if it refuses to waste its limited resources on the needy masses swimming in the water around it. But others say that if the poor are given a secure food supply, access to inexpensive health schemes and modest educational opportunities, then the rate of population growth will tend to decrease naturally. However, where aid programmes are implemented, lack of communications often means that the most needy are still not reached.

Western technology is available to help to solve this problem — but it must be technology of an appropriate

kind. In 1969 man stepped onto the moon; today many inhabited parts of our own planet still lack effective communications. Besides the skills that are needed in underdeveloped areas, there has to be the will to apply those skills in ways which do not hold out the promise of commercial profit or worldwide acclaim. Fortunately, there are those who are willing and able to use their creative genius to try to improve conditions for the poor and underprivileged in our world. One such man is Tim Longley.

The potential of hovercraft for linking isolated settlements was first realized soon after 1966 when Tim Longley went to Lake Chad as maintenance engineer for the Missionary Aviation Fellowship (MAF). MAF is an international Christian organization which operates a total of 110 light aircraft in twenty-two countries, in lifeline support of mission stations and clinics in some of the world's more remote areas. Many MAF pilots are former RAF personnel and friendly informal contacts between the two bodies have always been nurtured.

A Christian medical mission served the 250,000 people who lived around the shores or on the numerous floating islands of Lake Chad. The service was carried out by Dr David Carling, a British doctor of the Sudan United Mission, assisted by Africans based at clinics around the lake. The hospital launch, *Albarka*, had difficulty in getting to the clinics. The maze of more than 1,000 islands, the vast stretches of disease-ridden shallow water and the ever-changing level of the lake placed limitations on the use of motor boats, Land Rovers and MAF's amphibious Cessna aircraft. What was needed was an ambulance vehicle which could negotiate the lake's marshy edges. A hovercraft seemed the obvious solution.

On leave in Britain in 1969, Tim Longley surveyed the hovercraft market. He soon found that a craft of the right size for Lake Chad, which would operate at an acceptable cost, was not available. Tim, a qualified aircraft design engineer, who had headed a design team for the wings for the De Havilland Trident, began design work on a suitable craft. He was assisted by Tony Burgess whose skill as a hovercraft skirt designer was put to good use. They had only a limited budget, and since MAF had no production facilities, it seemed unlikely that the new 'Missionnaire' craft would ever get beyond the design stage.

Unknown to Tim, just a few miles from MAF's headquarters, Mike Ive, head of the technical department at Sir George Monoux Comprehensive School, Walthamstow, was looking for an innovative project to make maximum use of the school's newly-built workshop. The big doors were just wide enough to take the design — with only inches to spare — and the craft was built there by pupils, under Mike's direction.

The Royal Navy was so impressed with Missionnaire's performance and potential that their engineering yard at Gosport asked permission to build a second craft to act as a rescue vehicle on the mud flats of Portsmouth Harbour. On 29 July 1975, with a crew of four, Missionnaire left Lee-on-Solent at 0724 hours to circumnavigate the Isle of Wight. It arrived back two hours and fourteen minutes later. The approximate distance covered was sixty nautical miles, resulting in a block speed of twenty-seven knots. This record for lightweight hovercraft still stands.

Missionnaire was a success. But its use in Chad was now in question. The same severe drought which had taken me to Ethiopia in 1974 was proving much more prolonged in Chad. In 1976, the level of the lake was continuing to fall and large areas dried up altogether. Land Rovers could now be driven over these dry beds. Disappointingly, the sending of Missionnaire to Chad was postponed, and Tim was left to wonder what the purpose of his years of work had been.

Was Bill Gould's request for a hovercraft on the Kali Gandaki the answer? Was there a possibility that Missionnaire could be used in Nepal? Could it be transported to the Himalayas and would the craft which had been designed for use on the wide expanse of Lake Chad be controllable on the twisting, swirling river water of the Kali Gandaki?

A suitable craft would have to be inexpensive to purchase and maintain. It would have to exhibit abnormally good control characteristics, such as were not available in any of the present generation of light-weight hovercraft. And its components or sub-assemblies must be small enough for carriage in the light aircraft operated by MAF. For ease of maintenance, its construction would have to be based on motor car rather than aircraft technology.

On the road, when the going is too tough for a car, the Land Rover takes over. Tim was now seeking to design and build a 'River Rover' to operate where the normal boat had come to a full stop. This was a tall order and Missionnaire was clearly not suitable. Tim went back to his drawing-board. Soon the 'Hump' design (Hovercraft Utility Multi-Purpose) was taking shape: a simple, low-cost six-seater hovercraft, easily built from a kit, yet structurally robust and mechanically sound. Most significantly, the radical design of Hump's controls would enable it to be steered with the minimum of sideways skidding normally associated with hovercraft. This breakthrough was made possible by incorporating 'elevons', movable flaps just behind the driving propellers, allowing the hovercraft to bank on corners, greatly reducing the drifting. A simple device, but very effective.

The small back-street Gosport garage from which Tim Longley operates is singularly unimpressive. Tim himself is modest and quietly spoken. But what he lacks in facilities is more than made up for by application and single-minded determination, plus his in-

The life-expectancy of this pretty Nepali girl is very low.

novative germ of genius. British inventions of significance still come out of garages!

TEAR Fund, the organization with whom I had been involved when taking the drilling rig to Ethiopia, sponsored practical engineer Bernard Coleman to join the project on a full-time basis. TEAR Fund's objective is to show God's love in action by seeking to relieve two desperate areas of need in the world: to provide physical help with food, medicine, shelter and clothing, and to give spiritual direction and assurance by sharing the hope that belief in Jesus Christ can bring. They saw the long-term potential of the hovercraft project in helping developing countries, and sponsored Bernard in order to give Tim much-needed help with Hump's preparation and development.

Captain Beadon RN, Superintendent of the Royal Naval aircraft yard at Fleetlands, also appreciated the potential of the design and agreed that the prototype could be built as an apprentice training project, as an alternative to a second Missionnaire. The building of Hump began shortly after my return from Nepal in December 1975.

Tom Frank, the home secretary of British MAF, had been a strong supporter of the hovercraft project from the time of Tim's return from Chad in 1969. An 'ad hoc' action group was formed consisting of Tom Frank, Tim Longley, myself and Arthur Pont of the Bible and Medical Missionary Fellowship, the mission to which Dr Bill Gould at Tansen belonged. Our task was to pursue the goal of hovercraft communication for medical mission services in the Fourth World — the 'hovering doctor service'.

On 11 June 1976, the Joint Services Expedition Trust (formed in 1960 to encourage major expeditions) invited proposals from the three Armed Services for an exacting adventure. Such proposals would have to combine a project of scientific or technical value with a high level of public interest and opportunity for exacting personnel training, in order to be considered for the 9th Sponsored Expedition, in 1978-79.

Group Captain Peter Shelley, the RAF Director of Physical Education, had read a copy of my report on my visit to Tansen and the River Kali Gandaki. Only one of the Trust's previous sponsored adventures, the 1975 west-to-east crossing of the Sahara Desert by Squadron Leader Tom Sheppard, had had Royal Air Force leadership. It was about time for another. The director encouraged me to enter my hovercraft project for consideration. I had to report fast. Postpone, and the opportunity would be gone. My proposal just caught the 5 p.m. post on 30 November 1976. Exercise Kali-Cushion (as the expedition was later named) was born.

The Trust met on 18 February 1977. There it was decided that because River Rover was an untried design, it would be necessary for the Royal Navy Hovercraft Trials Unit to carry out an evaluation. It was also suggested that I should consider taking to Nepal an inflatable hovercraft, a Pindair 4, in addition to the River Rover. The French explorer, Michel Peissel, had used an earlier version of this craft on a number of Nepali rivers in 1972. I was also instructed to discuss the feasibility of the expedition with senior officers of the Royal Geographical Society. But, given satisfactory results in these investigations, it was likely that I would be given the coveted sponsorship.

The date set for the Royal Naval evaluation of the craft at Lee-on-Solent was 6 July 1977. The first 'flight' of Hump showed much promise, but as the trials date got nearer, the prototype developed faults. I asked for postponement of the evaluation and was told the Trust required a favourable report no later than 30 November 1977. Monday 19 September was fixed as the latest date for starting the evaluation to meet this deadline.

The first two weeks of September saw feverish activity in the Fleetlands workshops. At times it seemed that the long hours of working would be just so much wasted effort. The modifications included stretching the craft from its original length of 4.85 m to 5.6 m. With three days to go before the trials, performance improved slightly, but the craft remained far from satisfactory. Tim had run out of ideas. Over the weekend he thought of one or two minor adjustments, and with the feeling that he was clutching at straws, he incorporated these changes. After a quick lunch, we took the craft out on Portsmouth harbour again. Something amazing happened. She was no longer the same sick hovercraft. This time she just got up and went! Hump could now justifiably be renamed 'River Rover'.

Bearing in mind that no hovercraft had ever undergone an evaluation by the Royal Navy without previously having had months of vigorous testing in all conditions, it seemed impertinent that we should now head for the Hovercraft Trials Unit. I could not help feeling that the Royal Naval officers were mildly amused by our little craft. But its performance was impressive: just thirty-seven minutes from Fleetlands to Lee-on-Solent, only two minutes slower than the fastest time recorded by the larger and more powerful Missionnaire.

Once at Lee-on-Solent, despite poor weather conditions, the little craft never looked back. The use of the elevons to bank the craft round a series of buoys caught appreciative glances from the Navy's professional operators. At the conclusion the trials pilot, Lieutenant Commander Eric Palmer, warmly congratulated Tim on his very promising craft. Over lunch, Eric was positively enthusiastic about River Rover's performance. I hastened away to catch the London train and deliver the precious favourable report to the Ministry of Defence.

Sponsorship by the Joint Services Expedition Trust

consists of a grant to cover travelling expenses for the team and its equipment to the country of the expedition. It does not cover the cost of the purchase of the equipment — in this case the major budget item. This is the project leader's responsibility. With Trust sponsorship virtually assured, I was still therefore committed to raising £15,000 from supporters to cover the purchase of two River Rovers at £5,000 each, plus £3,700 for the inflatable Pindair 4 hovercraft. Against a background of world recession and inflation at home, the period 1977-78 was far from ideal for persuading firms to back our venture with financial assistance.

A few days after the trials were concluded, I met the board of the Missionary Aviation Fellowship to discuss the building of the two River Rovers for Nepal. Painful cuts were the order of the day for MAF, following a deficit in the budget for their worldwide flying operations. No further support from MAF funds would now be available. 'We regret that the River Rovers for Nepal will cost £10,000 each,' was the startling news I received.

After the elation of the Lee trials, I quickly came down to earth. I needed more money at a time when there was less of it around. My cash bill would now be nearly £27,500. After negotiation, I agreed to pay MAF £8,400 for each craft and be responsible for the supply of the engines and other major components. Hopefully I should get these items sponsored. Strange to relate, having boldly agreed to provide this money, I had peace of mind. But just *how* would the provision be forthcoming?

Earlier in 1977 my assistant at RAF Cosford, Flying Officer David Michael, had handed me a newspaper cutting which announced the Rolex Awards for Enterprise. Five prizes, each of 50,000 Swiss francs (at that time about £11,000), were offered to projects displaying initiative. One section included in the competition involved exploration and discovery. I had

With its simple bolt-together construction, River
Rover 01 was built in a tiny Gosport garage.

hopefully entered the proposed River Rover expedition. Rolex also received 3,000 other entries. Nevertheless, the arrival of a letter from the selection committee in Geneva quickened my expectations. Further detailed information on the hovercraft was required: the project was on the short list.

On 15 November 1977, a registered letter arrived from Geneva. I was declared a Rolex runner-up and awarded an Honourable Mention plus a specially engraved Rolex Chronometer. My high hopes for meeting a large part of the expedition budget from the Rolex Award were dashed.

Other startling news arrived. After twelve years of pioneering medical services, a change in family circumstances brought Dr Bill Gould home from Nepal. Tom Frank, too, gave up his post as home secretary of British MAF, and Group Captain Peter Shelley left the Royal Air Force to become an overseas director of the Save the Children Fund. Three men in strategic positions who had made much of the progress possible, had changed course.

On 13 December, however, I received the formal notification that the hovercraft expedition had been granted the sponsorship of the Joint Services Expedition Trust.

There is a school of thought which suggests that the planning of an expedition is more than half the fun. It is certainly a large part of the total effort. With just one year to lift-off for Nepal, three major hurdles remained: the budget, the team and the diplomatic clearance from Nepal. The first would be overcome by determination, time, hard work and providence. Careful selection would sort out the second obstacle, and patience the third.

The popular image of an expedition leader is of a brave man facing hardships and danger in inhospitable regions. Often an accurate picture; but he must also contend with much more petty and less glamorous situations! One of the most infuriating obstacles to forward progress is the complacency and defensiveness of many of the bureaucracies a leader has to tackle in order to promote his innovative ideas. Imaginative tactics and composite skills are called for. But for me the goal — River Rover's operation in the Fourth World — was a prize worth seeking, whatever the obstacles. In the event, the bureaucratic hassles were to prove far more exacting than the more obvious challenge of the tortuous rapids of the Kali Gandaki!

THREE

MONEY AND MEN

It was a year, less six days, to take-off and I had secured just £250 towards a fund-raising target of £27,500. Driving home to Ross-on-Wye, I was held up by motorway resurfacing work being carried out by Douglas Contractors. While I was stuck in the tailback of traffic, my thoughts wandered back to the halcyon days of Crusader canoeing and sailing camps which I had shared with John Douglas. It must have been at least sixteen years since I had last met John, who was now Managing Director of Douglas Contractors. I felt instinctively that with his nautical interest and Christian enthusiasm, John would warm to the hover-craft project. As soon as I got home, I wrote to him and by return of post was promised a generous donation. This was immediately matched by a similar one from BP Oil Ltd, who have been encouraging lightweight hovercraft design for many years.

Encouraged by this response, I now set out to get the support of the manufacturers of River Rover's components. Firms have a responsibility to their shareholders, and rightly require a return for their outlay of cash and components. A quickening interest and the promise of national publicity began to ensure that this return would be available. Indeed most suppliers caught the imaginative possibilities of the venture and backed us before seeking to justify such action commercially.

I had a video tape of the Lee-on-Solent trials to reinforce my initial written requests to the component manufacturers. I certainly tuned up my personal fitness, humping a large television set and video equipment up long staircases to show busy senior executives the capabilities of the craft. Time was short. I planned an eighteen-hour day. I wrote letters during evenings and early mornings and spent days on active promotion. I surprised myself with the productive possibilities of the early hours of the morning between 4 and 7 a.m. Many fruitful ideas came to me in the quiet hours before the dawn, as I sought God's guidance for the demanding day ahead.

In earlier discussion, the aims of the expedition had been examined at the Royal Geographical Society. I had been advised to take two River Rovers to Nepal so that a useful comparison could be made with the two jet boats used on the Nepalese rivers by Sir Edmund Hillary in 1965. Subject to solving problems of logistics, and obtaining finance and political permission, both the director of the RGS, John Hemming, and experienced explorer Robin Hanbury-Tennison felt that the basis of the expedition was a good one. Although the financial contribution from the RGS was modest, their support was, in effect, a certificate of competence which would do much to muster support from other sources.

One aluminium standard Hillman Imp (1000cc) sports engine had provided the power for the proto-type craft. This engine had performed well, but Tim Longley felt that we should give the production craft more power for the extremes of the tests which lay ahead in Nepal. Also, the British motor industry did not build an 80/100 brake horse power aluminium engine. The most important consideration in selection was a high power-to-weight ratio, plus an ability to withstand the corrosive action of sea water.

Tim selected the Renault 1647cc aluminium alloy engine — the same four-cylinder unit which drives the Renault 20TL saloon. At the company's UK headquarters at Park Royal, Tim and I met Renault engineer Len Paige. Len gave us many helpful suggestions, plus a little-used experimental 20TL engine, free of charge. The 20TL is a widely-used engine with a good reputation for reliability and the benefit of worldwide availability of spare parts. It is particularly suited to high revving over long periods in the kind of contrasting climatic conditions which exist in Nepal. The demands to be made of this engine were to be exceptional. From the moment the River Rover first hovered onto the Kali Gandaki, reliability would cease to be a subject of academic interest: it would become a matter of life and death for the crew.

When I had displayed my action video to Renault executives, they agreed to give one further engine and spares to the project. I agreed to purchase the third (spare) engine at a discount price. I said 'Goodbye,' they said 'Au revoir'; this was significant, as I was to realize later.

It is River Rover's construction which makes it so appropriate for use in the least developed countries of the world. It is based on low-cost, motor car technology with *Meccano* type bolt-together construction, largely of extruded aluminium angle sections and marine ply. All parts of the sub-assemblies are portable, in order to give low shipment costs and ease of repair. This is in distinct contrast to the high-cost aircraft-based technology of much present hovercraft manufacture.

The unique horizontally-hinged elevons and the framework for the whole craft were made of aluminium. In fact, the light but strong qualities of aluminium are the key to River Rover's construction. So, armed with plans and video tape, Tim and I set out for Banbury Cross and Alcan Aluminium. The managing director, John Kembery, probed our proposals with some searching questions. We left Banbury with Alcan's promise to provide all the costly aluminium needed for the two craft.

I had carelessly omitted my address from a letter to Lucas Industries, seeking electrical equipment for the craft. Lucas went to considerable lengths to locate me and offered all the electrical equipment needed, plus a generous donation. Instead of my letter being consigned to the waste-paper bin, a wealth of support reached the project. Kwikstik, the manufacturers of *Kwikseal*, essential to keep the craft watertight, provided both the material and a generous cheque.

Bearded Naval Commander Brian Holdsworth had been selected to lead the expedition's rear party. Brian informed me that his brother made luxury seating for vehicles. Paul Holdsworth and UOP Bostrom supplied specially-upholstered seating for the hovercraft, which made riding the rapids as comfortable as possible. A cheque towards the budget accompanied the seating.

The skirt and skirt fingers of a hovercraft equate to the tyres and tread of a motor vehicle. A gathering of apprentices greeted my arrival at the works of Northern Rubber at Retford. Young people are invariably receptive to new ideas, but both apprentices and senior management at Northern Rubber saw the potential of River Rover. This resulted in the company doing a special production run of their nylon neoprene material to make a gift of the required skirt-lengths.

Component manufacturers increasingly warmed to the project. RHP Bearings sent two engineers 250 miles from Doncaster to Gosport to ensure the correct fitting of the bearings they had given. Materials from

Maclellan fendering, International Yacht Paints, BRD couplings, Goodyear drive-belts, ICI perspex panels, Chubb fire extinguishers and Triplex windscreens were all willingly and freely supplied. These were the fruits of many miles' travel and long hours of proclaiming the possibilities of the vehicle. Delighted with this advance, I was able to forget the many cul-de-sacs which were an inevitable part of such an exercise.

Chief of the Defence Staff, Marshal of the Royal Air Force, Sir Neil Cameron, willingly agreed to be the patron of the expedition. As the pace of the preparations quickened, his wholehearted support was to be essential to the move forward.

It was now May Day 1978. With seven months to go, the budget still required £16,000 in cash. Ideally, the project needed one major sponsor. On 18 May, I attended the Rolex Enterprise presentation. From the hand of desert explorer Squadron Leader Tom Sheppard, I received my merit award watch. Grateful for the watch, I could not help reflecting on what might have been. So near — and yet still £16,000 away.

The other prime concern early in 1978 was the selection of the team. I had originally considered that twelve would be an adequate number. However, the Joint Services Trust encouraged me to expand on this, to give as many people as possible the chance of this unique experience. We now planned to take three hovercraft, a Gemini outboard inflatable craft and canoes, so it was possible to increase the numbers in the team: eventually twenty-six men were selected for Exercise Kali-Cushion.

Firstly, I needed people who would fit well into the team — people sympathetic to the humanitarian as well as the adventurous goals of the project. In a lonely river area, one lives under some strain, and the minor idiosyncrasies of one team-mate can grate on another. No team can afford a 'prima donna' who gets fractious,

The Red Arrows display team provide a fitting send-
off for Rover 01 as it leaves for Nepal.

or who is selfish or unpredictable. The Kali Gandaki needed a happy team who would enjoy working together.

Secondly, I needed candidates who possessed robustness of mind. They would have to withstand rigorous and hard physical work without fuss and endure mental strain, facing disappointment stoically. Thirdly, I needed to select on the basis of technical skills required for the expedition: engineer, doctor, pilot, signals expert, surveyor, logistics expert, linguist and canoeist.

In particular, I needed to recruit two representatives of that brave and efficient fighting force, the British Gurkhas. Their knowledge of custom and language, coupled with their devotion to duty, would make them invaluable members of the team. Unnecessary misunderstanding between the expedition members and Nepali villagers could be prevented by clear communication.

Finally, all team members would need to be physically fit and capable of trekking up to twenty miles a day in arduous terrain.

Flight-Lieutenant Paddy Gallacher, an Air Movements and Logistics Officer, had, unbeknown to him, been prepared for the role he was about to fill so enterprisingly. In 1974, he had been detached to Kathmandu for six months to be in charge of RAF flights during the Gurkha recruiting season. I had known Paddy since his Flight Cadet days at the RAF College Cranwell. His cheerful disposition and total commitment to the given task, coupled with proven knowledge of the intricacies of Nepali Customs and Excise organization, made his selection essential.

RAF Chief Technician Bruce Vincent, engineer and mountaineer, was another obvious choice, as I had personal knowledge of his qualities of resilience, resourcefulness and dependability. I appointed Bruce to take charge of engineering support.

Except for Tim Longley the designer, Paddy and Bruce, the balance of the team would be settled on the recommendation of others, followed by interview. I wanted a broad selection from the widest available field relying on the recommendation of those who knew the applicants' performance and compatibility at firsthand. Petty Officer Doug Couledge, who had many years' engineering experience at the Naval Hovercraft Unit was an early choice.

Royal Marine Corporal Tony Maher and Sergeant Rick Elliott of REME, the Royal Electrical and Mechanical Engineers, were the last UK-based service-men to join the team. Their contributions during those days of preparations were formidable. Rick painstakingly catalogued all the engineering spares likely to be needed and then equipped a lightweight portable workshop to be set up at base camp. His cheerful, likeable manner clearly impressed the suppliers of large quantities of free parts. Thanks to Rick, British Oxygen supplied the expedition with a field welding kit.

Royal Marines are trained to show the maximum initiative in any given set of circumstances. Tony Maher's imagination knew no bounds as he applied himself unreservedly to the task of providing the smaller items: sunglasses, dubbin, sweets for Nepali children appeared, along with all the little things which oil the wheels of a venture such as this. Tony also prepared the Navy's Gemini craft for transit and persuaded Johnsons' Marine to give the fuel tanks for River Rover. He then loyally wore a Johnson's jockey cap throughout the expedition.

This was Tony, thorough in detail and totally dedicated to the task in hand. He promoted the expedition in every direction. His father's Smithfield meat company gave the project a welcome cheque. I hardly dared think aloud in Tony's presence, as he was likely to act immediately on the mere hint of a suggestion.

His availability left me free to tackle the major out-standing tasks.

The 1/2nd King Edward VII's Own Gurkha Rifles (the Sirmoor Rifles) were garrisoned in Hong Kong. I flew to Hong Kong on 5 June to meet the two Gurkha Cor-porals provisionally selected to join the expedition.

The Gurkha is well-known for his martial excel-lence and for his devotion to his officer — the *sahib*. Arriving at the Burma Lines Officers' Mess in the New Territories, I placed my travelling-bag in my room. Returning a short while later, I found that my Gurkha orderly had unpacked for me. My pen lay neatly beside my notepad, and I smiled inwardly as I saw that he had also laid out all the bits and pieces I had accumulated at the bottom of my bag — rubber bands, old railway tickets and a dusty Remembrance Day poppy. Very late that evening, I sat alone in the mess ante-room. Suffering from jet-lag, my UK-oriented inner clock would not allow me to sleep. Hovering in the back-ground was my Gurkha steward. I took myself to bed: his devotion to his new *sahib* would otherwise have kept him up all night!

In the morning, I met the cheerful figures of Corporal Purnasing Gurung and Lance Corporal Shovaram Bura. Purna, a line boy and a second genera-tion Gurkha, was equally fluent in English and Nepali. Shov, his strong compact physique combined with a personal fearlessness, showed to a tee the qualities which make Gurkhas such dreaded opponents. Both had a unique contribution to make to Kali-Cushion and their selection was confirmed.

The high esteem in which the residents of Hong Kong hold both the Gurkhas and their mountain kingdom of Nepal is reflected by the generous resettle-ment schemes which have been financed from Hong Kong by private persons, notably brothers Sir Lawrence and Horace Kadoorie. This generosity was quickly extended to the hovercraft expedition, too. The Hong Kong-based shipping company of John Swire and Sons gave the project a handsome Hong Kong dollar cheque. But the full scope of their magnificent support would not be realized until a crisis point in the project in June 1979, some twelve months later.

A welcome cheque also came from the Hong Kong firm Dairy Farm and this was matched by one from Horace Kadoorie, the first contribution from a private individual. I was humbled by this generosity. How I appreciated this support from those who, at a very early stage, saw the potential of the craft. How much I wanted the Hovering Doctor Service to become a reality.

On 12 June I was back in England. The team was complete, but the question of finance and official clearance still remained. During my visit to Nepal in 1975, I had stood with Dr Bill Gould on part of the East/West Highway in the Terai (lowland region) which had been built and financed under the direction of the British Ministry of Overseas Development (ODM). I wondered if the ODM would be interested in my proposed contribution to the better communications of Nepal. I decided to share my ideas with the ministry. My letter outlining the proposed project struck a cord with Judith Hart, the minister at that time.

On 4 July 1978, I was invited to take my well-used video tape and proposals to the Science and Technology Department for evaluation. It was most refreshing to find that this was clearly one government department where action and decision were the order of the day! ODM Research scheme R3447 supported the hovercraft project with £7,000. In return one River Rover craft would be made available for ODM direction at the conclusion of the expedition. This craft, Rover 01, has now been earmarked for a medical support project on the Rio Apurimac in the Andes of Peru.

At the end of July, I was still awaiting formal diplomatic clearance from the Nepalese Ministry of Foreign Affairs. Our request was still bogged down in the higher realms of bureaucracy. A favourable answer had been expected for several months. I should continue to be patient and remain confident!

Then a signal arrived on 29 August: 'FROM: BRITDEFAT KATHMANDU ATTN SQN LDR COLE: MINISTRY OF FOREIGN AFFAIRS HAVE NO OBJECTION TO HOVERCRAFT EXPEDITION.' By the same post, a cheque for £7,000 came from the Ministry of Overseas Development. Two notable steps forward. And the third was the news that River Rover 01 would soon be ready for delivery.

Work on the production of the two expedition craft had begun at the small MAF Gosport garage-workshop in December 1977. Whilst Tim Longley was responsible for much of the design work, the assembly was very much a team effort. At the end of July 1978, experienced hovercraft engineer Tony Burgess and aircraft fitter Dennis Ling joined Tim and Bernard Coleman full-time to meet a fast-approaching deadline. Even the MAF secretary, Joyce Dewhurst, took time off from office duties to stitch together the rubber-coated nylon skirts and fingers of the craft. This MAF team, augmented in the later stages by members of the expedition during their leave and off-duty periods, enabled River Rover 01 to be completed by 18 September 1978. Thanks to dedicated effort, with much late evening and early morning work, River Rover 02 was finished in time for the departure of the expedition's rear party in January 1979.

On 25 September 1978 I received a letter from Jenny Cropper, the assistant producer of the BBC television programme *The World About Us*: 'I noticed your name and project on the list of the Rolex Awards for Enterprise, and I am very interested in your proposal to use a hovercraft in Nepal. *World About Us* is a weekly fifty-minute programme whose subjects range from wildlife to anthropology. The London-based production branch is concerned with people and expeditions.' The programme team wanted to cover the expedition.

Emotions are invariably roused on the subject of the practicability of hovercraft, so I welcomed the opportunity for an objective film assessment of the expedition. A producer and a cameraman could be included in the team without difficulty. However, the BBC decided to send a complete film crew: two cameramen, a sound recordist, assistant producer Jenny Cropper and director Tony Salmon.

The stereotype agreement which the BBC drew up for my signature asked me to be responsible for the safety of the film crew whilst on board the hovercraft, in accordance with Board of Trade regulations. I was quick to point out that regulations for operating hovercraft on previously unnavigable Himalayan rivers had yet to be written! With a wry smile, the BBC facilities department amended their form, accepting the risk to life which would be the lot of all.

I was concerned about taking a large self-contained group; personal relationships are always under pressure on expeditions and a group of five people reporting on us could easily complicate this aspect. But my fears proved to be groundless. The BBC crew fitted exceptionally well into the team.

The peak team strength was now thirty-one, plus a Nepalese liaison officer, a government requirement for all visiting film crews. On top of this we would employ cook boys plus, possibly, some local porters.

Early in October, the whole team gathered at the RAF Adventure Centre at Grantown-on-Spey, for three days' briefing interspersed with physical activity. Expedition doctors Donald Bruce and Robin

Dugdale inflicted us with the first of many injections against yellow fever, smallpox and rabies — the last being very painful. Our arms and seats were sore from this first assault.

The terrain of the area between the Cairngorms and Ben Macdhui is the largest and most varied arctic-type region in Scotland. In cheerful mood, the team climbed to the peak of Ben Macdhui (4296 feet). Most important, this exercise saw the first steps in moulding a team spirit. Fifteen miles of canoeing on the fast-flowing waters of the River Spey galvanized our thoughts towards the Kali Gandaki. Only the canoe experts in the team avoided an unscheduled swim. Mild by comparison with the obstacles ahead, this was a useful encounter and a foretaste of Nepal.

Hearing of our proposed venture, the elders of Grantown Baptist Kirk asked me to talk to the members and to a very attentive 5th Larbert Boys' Brigade. The after-church offering was a unique contribution to the expedition.

Mid-October 1978 marked the move of the biennial Motor Show from Earls Court in London to the new spacious premises of the National Exhibition Centre in Birmingham. On an earlier visit to the NEC, I had noticed Pendigo Lake strategically placed in front of the main entrance. As our River Rover was largely a product of motor car technology, I put to Dennis Collins, NEC's marketing executive, the idea of River Rover giving exhibition performances on the lake during the Motor Show. He welcomed the suggestion and I handed the details and the planning arrangement over to Tony Maher.

The Motor Show would be a remarkable opportunity to display the River Rover. From the initial sea trials we had been impressed by the smoothness of the engine and almost complete absence of vibration throughout the whole speed range. But we

On arrival at Kathmandu airport we could see the
spectacular Himalayas, and, in front, our destination
– the mountainous Middle Hills.

had a serious problem with the cooling system. We
had experienced overheating, and a series of minor
modifications had failed to solve the problem.

Tim Longley had precious little time to rectify this:

'I was sure of one thing; the craft could not possibly
perform at the Motor Show with the cooling troubles
we were experiencing. Two days before the start of the
show we decided to take drastic action. The radiator
was removed from its position ahead of the lift fan, and
re-positioned on the rear face of the lift-air collector
cowl, where it was cooled by pressurized lift-air
escaping through the radiator core to the atmosphere.
We worked through the night to complete this modification at 04.30 on the morning of 17 October. At
08.00 we began a prolonged static engine run with the
craft tethered. This time the engine settled down
comfortably to the prescribed working temperature of
85°C. It was just as well that it did, because at 09.00 a
crane arrived to lift the River Rover on to the flat truck
which was to transport it to the Motor Show.'

The craft arrived safely — and so did our two pilots.
I had been particularly fortunate in recruiting Captain
Gerry Bradman to the team. Gerry is the British
Army's most experienced hovercraft pilot, having
spent six years with 200 Squadron, driving heavy
SRN 6 craft in many parts of the world.

Peter Dixon's selection as a pilot was less obvious:

'Perhaps it seems strange that someone who had
never driven a hovercraft should be selected as one of
the pilots on an expedition such as ours. When I
learned of the expedition and its aims, through the
links maintained between Christians in the Services, I
immediately wanted to be involved in some way. However, not being the usual expedition type, I was not at
all sure what I could offer. After a great deal of prayer
and thought, I was convinced I should apply, and
Ingrid my wife was reconciled to the separation involved. Citing my experience as an RAF pilot, perhaps

of some value to the budding hovercraft pilot, I applied. There were hurdles, not least the fact that the Services do not lightly release their expensively-trained personnel for such expeditions, but at last I had my place in the team.

'"Gerry," Mike Cole had said, "I would like you to give Peter his first pre-expedition training on Pendigo Lake." When Gerry told me this, my mind instantly conjured up a remote stretch of water surrounded by jungle, or at least by Welsh hills. But this lake was man-made and located in the heart of the English Midlands. I was to receive my first instruction as a hovercraft pilot at the Motor Show! There I learned the basics of con-trolling a hovercraft; my introduction to rivers and rapids, shallows and rocks was not to come until we were on the Kali Gandaki itself.'

Public attendance at the Motor Show broke all previous records. Lake Pendigo was well placed for our hovercraft, with a contoured island on one side forming a channel, reminiscent of a narrow winding river. Gerry gave the long queues plenty to watch as he and Peter put River Rover through an eye-catching routine. BBC Television's motoring magazine programme from the Show opened with the editor arriving at the main hall in River Rover. The craft sped across the lake, then surged over the pebble beach and across the lawn to arrive at the main doors of the exhibition. An impressive performance.

Next day Tony Maher invited world champion racing driver, James Hunt, to inspect our craft. Articulate, provocative and uncompromising, James Hunt is a special celebrity and a particular attraction to both the public and the media. He now sat, dressed in tee-shirt and jeans on the River Rover, casually chatting to Tony Maher and REME engineer Mick Reynolds.

But there was nothing casual about the response of the motor car industry. Manufacturers were now seeking me out to ask if I could use this or that component on River Rover. As a result of the planned BBC film, Alan Dakers, Renault's UK Marketing Director, informed me that he was considering providing the major sponsorship. The end of the long trail to muster support was now in sight. The pieces of the varied jigsaw were all fitting into place.

The wide publicity brought to light a new question. The exceptionally fine control that the elevons gave the craft on the close confines of the exhibition lake had provoked great interest, and the advizability of taking out patents became clear. It would cost nearly £2,000 for patents to be raised in the principal hovercraft manufacturing countries of the world. I knew of trusts through which the Laing family had supported a variety of projects. I also knew that Sir Maurice Laing took a keen interest in nautical activities, particularly sailing, and in Christian endeavour. Feeling that bold action was required, I wrote to Sir Maurice. He generously provided the necessary finance for Missionary Aviation Fellowship to secure patents.

Having boosted the total operating time to thirty-eight hours, the craft was transported from Birmingham to London to the headquarters of the Royal Geographical Society. There, on 1 November, some 250 supporters and well-wishers, including the Nepalese ambassador, attended a valedictory meeting to wish the expedition success. Under floodlighting in the garden, Gerry briefly operated River Rover to give those present a glimpse of its capabilities. Faces appeared at the windows of the select, well-appointed flats overlooking the garden, expressing obvious surprise at these goings-on on such revered territory.

Bathed in the floodlights, Alan Dakers handed over a canary-yellow Renault cheque to close the fund-raising quest. Full provision at the eleventh hour! Collecting my notes from the main lecture theatre, I glanced up at the coving in the ceiling carved with the names of the famous explorers of the last 150 years. Prominent on this roll were the names of Baker, Grenfell and Livingstone, men who had combined adventure with Christian incentive.

FOUR

TO THE FOURTH WORLD

On 2 November 1978, advance party leader Major
Dennis Cooper left for Kathmandu. En route in Hong
Kong, he was joined by Lieutenant Neil Fisher of the
Queen's Gurkha Signals and REME engineer Corporal
Ben Bennett.

When a Gurkha recruit joins the British Army he is
taught to read and write Roman Urdu or Gurkhali in
English letters. The 'father' of the team, fifty-four-
year-old Dennis Cooper, had spent his previous tour of
duty teaching these recruits in Hong Kong. After many
years as Army squash champion, Dennis is the current
veterans' champion, and is still able to beat the
reigning full champion on occasions. His personal
physical fitness plus his language skills made him the
ideal leader of the advance party. Dennis had spent his
childhood in India during the declining years of the
British Raj. We were to be particularly impressed by
his skill in using the 'carrot and stick' method to
handle the very individually-minded Sikh drivers of
the battered Tata trucks, used to take our craft to Base
Camp.

Lieutenant Neil Fisher, who had been serving in

Brunei, would team up with Lieutenant John Rollins to provide our essential radio communications. It would be his task to confirm the outline permission which we had already received to use our equipment. Radio communication is a sensitive area and permission from the Nepalese Government to operate independently is not lightly given.

REME engineer Ben Bennet, serving in Hong Kong, also joined the advance party. He was to team up with fellow REME members Rick Elliott and Mick Reynolds. As an RAF officer, I was largely ignorant of the wide range of the professional skills that they possessed. Their efforts at improvization in the field were to prove invaluable.

Ever since the earliest travellers went to Nepal, strangers entering or leaving the country have been confronted with various forms of administration which they just seek to satisfy. These practices are still going strong and 'permission letters' were certainly needed in 1978, particularly for a strange craft that floats on air! Dennis, Neil and Ben went ahead to smooth the trail. They spent most of their time in Kathmandu trying to obtain trekking permits, visa extensions, road permits, and import licences, in hiring vehicles and employing Sherpas. They also made two journeys into the hills and picked a site for our Base Camp at Ramdighat.

Gurkha Corporals Purnasing Gurung and Shovaram Bura had already travelled to Nepal in September to spend some well-earned leave with their families before joining the advance party in Kathmandu. Their particular task would be to ensure that our friendly ties with the Nepalis were correctly maintained — with due reference to cultural demands: boots off in Nepalese homes, no eating with the left hand, no starting major journeys using Sherpas on a Tuesday — an inauspicious day.

In preparation for the variety of tasks that are undertaken worldwide by RAF C130 Hercules aircraft, a monthly global training flight is scheduled. Our hovercraft would make an unusual cargo and our destination at Kathmandu was certainly off the main route of airways. Excellent training value! A tentative promise had been made to the expedition for the November training flight, leaving the UK on 20 November 1978. At the beginning of November, this flight was reallocated to other tasks.

I wrote informally to the expedition's patron, Sir Neil Cameron, expressing my concern at this delay. The aircraft allocaters informed me that they hoped to route the December trainer through Kathmandu, but that writing to the Chief of the Defence Staff would not affect the issue one way or the other. Had I over-reacted? The preparations of four years were nearing completion and my single-minded concentration was fixed on the immediate goal. Our departure had been carefully timed to coincide with the start of the post-monsoon period. However, with my knuckles duly rapped, I received the following details:

ASCOT Flight 5406 the December trainer

	LYNEHAM	081030 (10.30 a.m. on 8 December
081600	ATHENS	090835
091500	BAHRAIN	100730
101130	BOMBAY	110500
110905	KATHMANDU	

The last weeks up to 8 December were spent preparing the hovercraft and equipment for air freight, with Paddy Gallacher's eagle eye inspecting every item for correct packing and labelling. On the evening before departure from RAF Lyneham, Donald Bruce and Robin Dugdale attacked us again with syringes full of anti-hepatitis gamma globulin and anti-rabies vaccines.

The Kali Gandaki has dug a deep valley in the high hills of West Nepal.

Using up the fuel in River Rover's tank prior to venting for air transit, Gerry Bradman gave an impressive performance of the craft's capabilities on the smooth surface of the airfield's perimeter track. The pilots of the Red Arrows, practising for their next display season, swooped down, spilling their coloured vapours to salute River Rover prior to the loading on to the Hercules.

On seeing the formidable pile of equipment stacked in the hangar, the duty movements clerk assured us that the aircraft would be 'bulked out' before half of it had been loaded. Providentially, the duty engineer was Alan Cutler, who had, unknown to me, followed the progress of our venture for some time. He authorized the off-loading of an additional Hercules spare wheel. We were grateful for this positive help, which released more needed freight space. Paddy worked all night, carefully making maximum use of the space available. There was a triumphant, if a little weary, note in Paddy's 'All aboard' at early breakfast.

After bidding farewell to the main party who were flying out by RAF VC10 to Hong Kong and then on by Thai International Airlines to Kathmandu, Peter, Paddy and I departed from RAF Lyneham with hovercraft and crated equipment. We left behind us a wet and cold British morning, and also our families, who were about to face the worst British winter for decades.

Although the hold of a Hercules filled with nine tons of freight is not the most comfortable of passenger compartments, we were relieved to be on our way. Since the three of us were the only passengers, the Captain, Flight Lieutenant Dai Davies, and his crew treated us as 'honorary crew members' and we were spared most of the airport processing usually suffered by passengers on an impersonal airliner. We had three brief over-night stops. In Athens, we became hopelessly lost in the narrow streets of the Plaka district below the Acropolis. In Bahrain, we saw the contrast between giant oil tankers and tiny dhows, between luxury hotels and the simple Arab dwellings around them, and in Bombay we lost most of our ground time to the hilariously inflexible airport bureaucracy.

The fourth day's flight took us north over Delhi, where the air-way turned sharply to the east. Half an hour later, over the Indian city of Lucknow, we caught sight of the Himalayas, and I was soon able to pick out the Annapurna massif 150 miles to the north, flanked by the lone peak of Dhaulagiri. I knew that between the two lay the upper reaches of the Kali Gandaki river. We strained our eyes to catch a glimpse of Everest.

All this makes it sound as though we were heading for the Switzerland of the East. In reality we were on our way to one of the poorest countries in the world. The poverty of the people is often belied by the cheerful way they bear their crippling difficulties. Four out of ten infants die before the age of five, and life expectation is less than forty years. Broken bones are rarely set properly and wounds frequently turn gangrenous. Victims of leprosy are as socially unacceptable today as they were in biblical times. The tubercular cough punctuates the dawn chorus of every Nepali village. We were about to land in an area rightly labelled the 'Fourth World'.

A turbulent descent brought us to Kathmandu airport. As we emerged from the plane into the bright sunlight, gazing at the snow-capped mountains, Dennis Cooper and Neil Fisher were there to greet us. We were informed that the worldwide C130 fleet was being temporarily grounded as each aircraft returned to base, following a crash in the USA. The timing of our departure had been precisely right!

Paddy had cause to remember our arrival at Kathmandu:

'We had left Bombay in mid-morning. The aircraft was clammy and uncomfortable. Six hours later we were on the approach to Tribhuvan Airport. I didn't look out to admire the green carpet of rice fields or to wonder at the ancient-looking pagodas rising above the cluttered rooftops of Kathmandu. As Mike and Peter clicked their cameras, I looked at the jumble of freight straining under the cargo nets and wondered what reaction it would provoke amongst the Nepali customs officials. As the aircraft rumbled along the taxi-way, I thumbed through the manifests for the hundredth time. Dennis Cooper had telexed us two days before we left England, warning us that we must be prepared to pay a 25 per cent deposit on all freight being imported to Nepal.

'Our equipment had been conservatively valued at over £70,000. There was no question of our funds being able to stretch to an additional £15,000 at this stage in events. On the other hand, we knew that a recent mountaineering expedition had had to be cancelled because it was unable to obtain customs clearance for its stores. Our manifests listed several restricted articles — radio kit, cameras, medical drugs — all items likely to arouse the suspicions of a government sensitive to its position as a buffer state, sandwiched between two relative super-powers, India and China.

'As the large cargo door of the Hercules eased open, a large group of airport workers gathered round the aircraft to see what hidden treasures were stored in its hold. I saw Dennis at the back of this crowd struggling to reach the door.

'"Paddy!" His normally cheerful voice was uncharacteristically shrill. "This is the Chief Customs Officer, Mr Thapa." I shook hands with a thin, angular man in traditional Nepali dress. "He wants to know how much of the equipment is being left in Nepal."

'"Why?" I snapped, rather unreasonably. "It's all government property and the Queen wants it back as soon as the expedition is over!" Surprisingly, Thapa seemed to appreciate this logic and nodded. "You have consumables, no?" he retorted wrily.

'"Yes," I admitted.

'"Come this way," said Thapa.

'Dennis and I followed him through a dusty shed full of uncleared air freight into a shabby little office. We listened helplessly as he and four other officials studied our manifests and jabbered away in Nepali. Eventually he scribbled some calculations and, turning to Dennis said, "You must pay 5,600 rupees."

'With almost indecent haste, Dennis counted out the money and, with a perfunctory "Namaste" we quickly left the room with our by now quite grubby manifests.

'"Dennis—5,600 rupees is £250 isn't it?" I said incredulously.

'"That's right!" he grinned. Let's get that gear off quickly before they change their minds!"'

So that Flight 5406 could continue on its way the next morning, we had to unload the Hercules in the short time left before dusk. No freight-moving equipment was available, and we shifted the hovercraft and equipment onto the tarmac with the aid of a very willing team of airport porters.

Our business in Nepal's capital city demanded haste — we had yet to tune into the Nepali pace of life. There were customs formalities to complete and bureaucratic tangles surrounding temporary imports to be unravelled. We hired a taxi but the meter had broken down — not an unusual occurrence. Other means of transport could be had in Bike Street. For eight rupees a day (25p), Paddy had found a convenient, if hazardous method of getting round the city.

But we did have part of one afternoon to explore Kathmandu. The city gets its name from the Temple of Kastha Mandap, a pagoda said to have been constructed from the timbers of one tree. The city lies towards the western end of a large, broad valley, surrounded by wooded hills. Several snow-capped peaks of the high Himalayas are visible in the distance. The old city centre has retained much of its medieval character, though now encircled by new development and choked with tourists and souvenir shops. Newly-arrived Tibetan refugees rub shoulders with the cosmopolitan colony of visitors from the inquisitive West. The magnificent pagoda temples, the houses and shops share a rich legacy of intricate, sometimes somewhat obscene wood carvings — a contrast with the dirty streets, open sewers, urban cattle and throng of people.

Peter Dixon recorded his immediate impressions on this, his first visit to Kathmandu:

'If I had thought that we could spend the forty-eight hours before the arrival of the main party as tourists in Kathmandu, I was mistaken. Our tasks — mine was to transform the River Rover from a piece of air-freight into an operational hovercraft — took up most of the time. Nevertheless, one does not need leisure to establish first impressions of a place. The glamour associated merely with the name "Kathmandu" builds up expectations to the point where the reality is inevitably an anticlimax. Whatever I had expected from Nepal's capital, the mild disappointment I felt came largely from the impression that we had arrived ten or twenty years too late. Twentieth-century civilization had made its mark on a place which had once been isolated and unique. To be sure, signs of the old way of life were still evident. Alongside a Chinese-built truck on the modern metalled highway trudged a file of simply-attired porters, carrying back-breaking loads to some remote destination. Progress along the roads was continually interrupted by cows, pigs or even people strolling casually in front of vehicles; the humans seemed to have even less road-sense than the animals! And yet the mere existence of the roads gave me a sense of having been cheated.'

Having cleared the launch site, Rover 01 was carefully let down to the river at last.

In the trading area of Hanuman Dhoka we got a glimpse of the age-old Kathmandu. In this setting each Nepali pursues the hand skills of his craft. These are the poor, whose daily concerns are the next meal and their religion. To them the surest security is the protection and favour of their gods. Gods are carved on doorways, windows and on the walls of every house and often smeared with vermillion or scattered with stale cooked rice. Throughout each day the individual gives his respect to the multitude of gods in numerous ways. There is no shortage of people in Kathmandu and there seem to be at least as many gods. Although Hinduism is the state religion, Lumbini in the Terai is the birthplace of the Buddha, and this has resulted in a unique blend of the two religions, only found in Nepal. 'Are you a Hindu or a Buddhist?' The answer — 'We worship at all the shrines.' Alongside these religions of the East there is also a handful of Christians.

In 1846 a nobleman Jung Bahadur Rana massacred in one evening more than 100 potential rivals and brought in the isolationist Rana rule which was to last in Nepal for 104 years. The nominal Shah kings were powerless in their palaces. In 1950, five leaders secretly approached the king to discuss possible reform. They were labelled traitors. Two were hanged publicly, two were shot and the fifth, a Brahmin (the priestly caste and therefore unable to be executed), was given life imprisonment. Today these men are national heroes and the Martyrs' Arch is a prominent feature in Kathmandu.

The first democratic stirrings of the Nepalese people had taken place. In 1951, after centuries as the closed land of mystery, revolution opened Nepal to the influence of the outside world. King Tribhuvan undertook ambitious plans of sweeping reforms. Help from outside was welcomed. Hundreds of foreigners arrived to staff various kinds of aid and development programmes.

Into this situation individual Christians and missions were welcomed. However, evangelistic work was not permitted and conversion was forbidden by law. To the west of Nepal in India, Dr Bob Flemming was principal of Woodstock School and his wife Bethel was the school doctor. Bob had a personal interest in the study of the birds of the Himalayas. He wanted to extend this study into Nepal and he was surprised when, in 1949, permission to visit was granted. Accompanying him on subsequent trips went his wife and medical missionaries Carl Taylor and Carl Fredericks, who, during their travels, dispensed medical supplies to the people. This led to the start of mission-led medical work in Kathmandu and the founding of the hospital at Tansen.

Under clear blue skies in November 1952, six European ladies and five Nepali Christians made a trek from the Indian border at Nautanwa to the mountains they had viewed from afar for many years. At Pokhara they erected pre-fabricated aluminium huts which they had brought with them from India. Because the buildings shone in the sun this was soon labelled the 'Shining Hospital'. The hospital soon became a landmark, famous for its dedicated life-saving work not only for the local populace but also, later, for the many European trekkers caught in distress on the trails to the northern 'Mustang' area.

From my home area in North London, Dr Pamela Dodson joined the mission medical team in Nepal in 1953. On many a Sunday my Bible Class leader would read from a crumpled airmail letter, speaking of Bhatgaon, of Gorkha, of the mountain-top hospital at Tansen, and reporting on Pam's activities. As a young man, these had been just vague names to me. As I gathered with missionary personnel in Kathmandu in mid-December 1978 and listened again to reports of Gorkha, of Tansen and of the generator needed at the remote dispensary in the east at Okhaldungha, I realized that my subconscious had been prepared some twenty-four years previously in that Bible Class. I now found myself explaining our aspirations for River Rover to the missionaries and distributing Christmas cards and gifts from relatives in the UK.

Earlier that day the orchid-bedecked main party had arrived in a DC8 of Thai International Airways, giving Dennis more occasion to organize us. He had been particularly fortunate in hiring a Mercedes mini-bus (left over from an overland expedition from Germany) for the team to travel in, and two trucks, one for equipment and the other for the hovercraft. The loading and lashing down of the hovercraft were completed with relatively little difficulty; the truck had to be 'modified' with hacksaws, but its Sikh owner-driver seemed unconcerned.

The convoy's departure from Kathmandu gave us a splendid example of the Nepalese pace of life. The schedule called for a departure at 8 a.m.; by 9.30 a.m. the convoy was finally on the road. At 10.15 a.m. we arrived back at our starting point, having lost contact with one of the two trucks. Finally, however, all three vehicles were under way on the two-day road journey to our Base Camp at Ramdighat. Every few miles along the road we came to a district boundary, where we had to stop to pay a road toll. Children clamoured around the windows, selling tangerines, small bananas and peanuts.

Climbing up to the rim of the Kathmandu valley and into the Middle Hills is like passing into another country. The hills are steep and rugged, the streams and rivers twist tortuously, seeking a passage on their way to top up the flow of the sacred giants. There is only one road to the west in an area the size of southern England, and this fact, coupled with the rough mountain terrain, has left the people of the Middle Hills in isolation, locked in the remote interior. It is only as one penetrates into the hills that the true character of the people and the hardships with which they contend can be observed. They follow a simple subsistence lifestyle and pray to the gods that catastrophes of disease and famine will pass them by. The villagers have carefully terraced the hillsides to gain the maximum possible area for planting their precious lifepreserving crops. They are utterly dependent on the next harvest. Their faces and bodies show the effects of the hard labour of carrying everything on their backs. The happenings in Kathmandu valley belong to another world.

At every stop we had to tell the obstinate truckdrivers to go more slowly; the condition of the road to Pokhara was something most of us had never before experienced. It showed how difficult it is to maintain communications in such terrain. The construction was carried out under Chinese direction without sophisticated road-building equipment, relying heavily on mass unskilled labour. The combination of soft unstable rock and earth with a monsoon climate ensures that there are frequent landslides. At intervals along the way we would see large gangs of labourers dressed in rags, shifting rocks or resting in the austere shelters they had built for themselves.

About two-thirds of the way from Kathmandu to Pokhara (125 miles/200 kilometres), we rounded another blind bend to find a small crowd staring into the valley below. Two hundred feet below us we saw a public bus lying upside-down among the trees. Although from its condition I thought it must have been there for months, the bus had in fact gone over the edge about half an hour earlier, with forty-one passengers aboard. We were to learn that rust and dilapidation was normal for a 'road-worthy' bus.

First on the scene had been some Australians, taking an old London double-decker bus on the overland route from England. While the local Nepalis stood

immobile and shocked, the Australians had carried
the injured back up to the road. We were to experience this implicit trust in a white face in an emergency
frequently in the coming months.

Donald and Robin immediately set to work, admin-
istering pain-killers and covering wounds. The rest of
us helped as best we could; Tony Maher's Royal Marine
first aid training was put to good use. The different
requirements of the Fourth World were brought
home. Robin soon found himself running out of
syringes for injections; without thinking, he had been
discarding the sterile disposable syringes as he
normally would in a well-equipped Western hospital.
Women refused to uncover any part of the anatomy
between calf and neck. The injured lay stoically by the
roadside in extreme pain, without complaint or any
sound. When trucks were commandeered as ambu-
lances, many patients were unwilling to be taken to
hospital. This was puzzling, until it occurred to us that
there was possibly, for each of them, a small bag on top
of the crippled bus containing most of their worldly
goods. My allocated task was to comfort a dying
woman who was spasmodically spitting blood. I held
her hand and witnessed the failing pulse. She remained calm and uncomplaining. In the midst of this
rescue operation, two Chinese trained in first aid
(known as 'barefoot' doctors) arrived to assist. They
were attached to the local Chinese-funded road-
building team. They did not seem out of place as they
quickly set to work stitching wounds with British
Service equipment, using sign language to communicate with Donald and Robin. In spite of the great
cultural divide, a pressing emergency had caused
these two brands of 'medicine men' to work together.

Dr Donald Bruce describes this incident:

'As Robin stitched, I examined each survivor and
established a priority for their evacuation by open
truck to the nearest hospital, four hours' drive away at

Pokhara. I subsequently learned that of the forty-one passengers, four had died and three had sustained multiple fractures. The majority had escaped with only minor cuts and bruises. The other expedition members assisted with cleaning and carrying, but it was a rather subdued party that continued westwards.'

Surprisingly, the number of serious injuries was small. We later learned that bus crashes were a regular occurrence, and that a bus which was well packed with passengers rarely produced many serious injuries. The moral: never climb on to a Nepalese bus unless it is already full. The bus driver was taken away to jail, since he had jumped from the bus when a collision had seemed imminent, leaving it to dive straight over the cliff! One of our Sikh drivers, I was told, was a distant relative of the man in jail. He provided food and a blanket for this unfortunate fellow. Drivers are automatically held responsible for any injury occurring in a motor accident, whatever the cause. His position could have been worse, for had he killed a sacred cow, he could have expected a longer prison sentence.

This episode did much to discourage the team members from attempting to drive road vehicles. I hoped that sacred cows would give the River Rover a wide berth. And I wondered if our insurance broker was fully aware of the variety of risks his policy for the expedition might be expected to cover!

Having done all we could, the convoy took to the road once more. After multiple delays, an overnight stop at Pokhara was now inevitable. Arriving there in the dark, we found a dull and unimposing town with few distinctive features. But next morning, as the sun rose to disclose the magnificent peaks of the Annapurna massif and the pyramidal shape of Machhapuchhare towering high above us, we realized that Pokhara's main attraction is its location. Although the Annapurna peaks are higher, it is the closer Machhapuchhare which is the more impressive. The derivation of its name, meaning 'fish-tail', is not obvious unless one is some days' walk west of Pokhara, when its twin peaks become clearly visible.

We stayed that night at the International Nepal Fellowship's Shining Hospital. The fortunate few slept at the home of Peter Hitchin, the hospital's administrator, while the rest had to be content with the hard, but welcome, floor of the hospital's dining room. During the evening, Peter described the hospital's work to the expedition's two doctors. Started originally as a general hospital, the Shining Hospital now specializes in the treatment of leprosy and tuberculosis work, since there is now also a Government hospital at Pokhara. An important activity is the training of paramedical teams who travel on foot to remote villages surveying the incidence of these diseases and giving initial treatment. Knowing at firsthand the difficulties of travelling in a region not served by roads, Peter showed great interest in our hopes to develop a mean of transport for remote areas.

Shortly after 8 a.m. the convoy set out on the final four-hour leg of the journey to Ramdighat. We drove past the airfield and Pokhara's beautiful lake, and soon left the flat valley as the road took to the hills once more. After a while the road followed the path of the Andhi Khola, a tributary of the Kali Gandaki river, and we stopped at intervals to investigate possible launching sites for the River Rover. Dennis and Neil had advised us that the drop in river level would make a launch at Ramdi difficult and it seemed wise to look for other possibilities while we had the chance. However, none of the sites seemed suitable.

Leaving the Andhi Khola valley, the road started to approach the top of a wooded ridge. At last, as we rounded a sharp bend, I turned to the team.

'Gentlemen, the Kali Gandaki!' I said excitedly — sounding, I suppose, like a courier on a coach tour.

The vicious rapids of the Kali Gandaki would have made operation of most craft completely impossible.

There, 3,000 feet/900 metres below, was the river we had come to meet, looking wide and calm from our elevated viewpoint. As the steep, winding road descended towards the steel bridge at Ramdighat, we were able to distinguish more detail, to pick out rapids and possible paths through them. Finally we turned down a dirt track and saw, behind ruined buildings, the drab green tents our advance party had erected. This was Base Camp.

The Kingdom of Nepal lies on the southern slopes of the Himalayan mountains, squeezed between China and India. Rectangular in shape, it is about 500 miles/800 kilometres from west to east, varying between 56 miles/90 kilometres and 143 miles/238 kilometres from north to south. A land of paradox, of great variety and cultural interest, the scenic beauty is however marred by pressing problems and individual distress.

The highest snow-capped peaks in the world mark the northern border. On the southern border is the lowland tropical alluvial strip of land called the Terai which merges naturally into the North Indian Plain. To the north of the Terai stand two mountain ranges. The Siwalik rises from the jungle plains to reach an altitude of 5,000 feet/1,520 metres. The formidable Mahabharat Lekh range, with certain peaks reaching 10,000 feet/3,000 metres, lies as a complete chain across the country further to the north. This barrier has a dramatic effect on the whole river system of the country. The central hills complete the picture, forming a broken, undulating area which merges into the Himalayan slopes. Eight of the mighty south-flowing rivers rise in Tibet and cut their way south through the Himalayan chain, following deep valleys and gorges.

These rivers wash the ankles of Everest, Lhotse, Kanchenjunga, Annapurna and Dhaulagiri, the world's mightiest peaks. On reaching the formidable

Mahabharat barrier, the rivers change course, flowing east or west seeking a gap through to the Terai to link with the Ganges. Having successfully penetrated the Himalayas, the rivers funnel into just three exits to escape the Mahabharat, just like a crowd at a football match seeking the exits when the final whistle is blown.

The greatest and most spectacular of these rivers is the Kali Gandaki — called by the Nepalis the 'Goddess of Death'.

Our base at Ramdighat was the bridging point where the one and only road of west Nepal crosses the mighty Kali Gandaki in the heart of the massive Mahabharat mountain range. The source of the Kali Gandaki lies deep inside Tibet. Performing a geographical miracle, it flows south for seventy miles *against* the slope of the north face of the high Himalayas. Its waters pass through a wide variety of types of climate and vegetation on its spectacular route to the plains of India. The river cuts across Nepal's sensitive border and in a belt thirty miles wide, where entry is forbidden to the foreigner, the river briefly changes its name to the Mustang Khola. The waters of the north-flowing tributaries cascading downhill from the Himalayan slopes now remarkably change to a southerly direction on reaching the Kali Gandaki.

Flowing through the alluvial soils of the northern plateau area, the river now cuts the Himalayan breach, forming the deepest canyon in the world. This cutting reaches nearly three miles in depth over a length of four miles. The canyon is set in the Himalayan rain-shadow, and this has deprived the gorge of the monsoon rains which would turn this placid stretch of water into a spectacular torrent. However, the eye-catching cataracts of the next eighteen miles, as the river falls nearly 5,000 feet, more than make up for this deficiency. Here, the vicious, swirling Kali Gandaki plunges down the steep 'staircase' with an unrelenting roar.

The remaining south-flowing section of the river between Beni and Riri Bazaar is punctuated by frequent rapids, but hovercraft navigation could well be possible here. If so, a proposed hydro-electric scheme for the riverside town of Baglung would certainly benefit. At Riri, having breached the Himalayas, the mighty river is turned east, seeking to find an escape route through the formidable Mahabharat Lekh. The eighty-five mile stretch of river between Riri Bazaar and Narayanghat, in the Terai, was to be the prime target for our expedition team and the River Rovers.

The effort nature had expended in turning the river had created a series of severe rapids over the fifteen miles between Riri and our base at Ramdighat. This was the track to test River Rover to its limit. From Ramdighat to Narayanghat there are seventy miles of fast-flowing, rapid-strewn, previously unnavigable water, between the only (often impassable) road in the Middle Hills and the new East-West Highway in the Terai. The expedition would seek to operate the craft regularly up and down this part of the river in support of a pilot community health scheme. The river is the only possible means of communication in a large area where disease and poverty are rife. A visit to the one mission hospital, high in the hills at Tansen, often involves many days of laborious trek. Would our machines prove to be craft of appropriate technology, bringing the promise of a better quality of life to the peoples of this isolated area tottering on the brink of disaster?

The river track for our operations would be governed by the weather conditions. From October until the following May the days are clear and rain-free, with the exception of a brief period of winter rains in January. During this period it is warm during the day (up to 75°F/24°C) and cool in the morning and evening (around 40°F/5°C). Below 10,000 feet the temperature rarely falls to freezing-point. December and January are the coldest months; February and March bring warmer weather and towards the end of March haze obscures mountain views, and daytime temperatures may reach 90°F/32°C.

The pre-monsoon period begins in late April or early May. Heavy clouds gather and thunderstorms occur in the evening. Heavy rain, mist and fog accompanied by frequent landslides make all aspects of travel difficult during the monsoon period from June to the end of September.

Whilst fast-flowing water is not an obstacle to River Rover, the debris carried by the flood-waters is a notable hazard. I considered it practicable to be able to navigate River Rover on the Kali Gandaki from October to May. As the waters drop, the river operations by hovercraft get progressively more difficult as rocks are uncovered and rapids get steeper. From December 1978 to March 1979 a track of ever-increasing difficulty would test our team and their machines to the limits of their performance.

Almost four years ago to the day, I had stood at Ramdighat with Bob Abbott. I now offered a silent prayer of thanks. Many hurdles had been surmounted. Four years of continuous snakes and ladders, with the ladder just reaching to the next objective, often at a faith-testing eleventh hour, lay behind me. And I was now on the brink of the actual adventure that all this had been leading up to.

In human terms, expedition leadership is a lonely occupation. With the preparation over, I was now responsible for twenty-five highly motivated, single-minded individuals and a craft of new technology, depending on a long line of logistics in one of the poorest countries of the world. A sharp reminder of this awaited me on the river's bank.

Base Camp had been laid out on military lines by the advance party, and the luxury of arriving at a prepared site was greatly appreciated. Dennis' patience with the truck drivers had lasted well, so to facilitate their early release we immediately started unloading. The hovercraft truck was reversed down the track to the beach, some thirty feet above river level, and about twenty of us lifted the hovercraft down on to the sand.

That done, we sat down, relaxed and had our first cup of hot, sweet, Sherpa tea. We drank, contemplating the sight in front of us — would we be able to launch? Although our route to the river was blocked with rock, I was convinced that Ramdighat was the best launching-site. Drawing on my geographical training, I reasoned that as Himalayan rock is geologically young, it should break up with sufficient perseverence. The majority of the team disagreed with me. In any case the obstacles were formidable.

Peter Dixon recalls the incident:

'I think most of us felt that it would be impossible to launch safely at Ramdi, but Mike Cole, with characteristic confidence, had insisted on unloading the hovercraft and paying off the drivers. We were committed, but at first the task looked hopeless. The craft sat atop a high sandbank which sloped steeply towards the river; at the bottom were ten-foot rocks forming the river's bank. In one place, however, there was an eleven-foot gap whose floor was covered with relatively small rocks. A launch *might* be possible, we decided, but only after extensive "modification" of the terrain. Pickaxes, shovels and crow-bars emerged from the boxes of equipment, and we started two days of shifting sand, moving rocks that would move and breaking ones that would not. All this was under a burning sun — in mid-December. Plywood panels were laid over the remaining rocks to protect River Rover's hull and at last, to Mike's relief, we were ready to launch. Mike had been getting visibly more impatient as the slow preparations proceeded, waiting to see the event he had been planning for four years — River Rover on the Kali Gandaki.'

In 1965, Sir Edmund Hillary and his New Zealand companions had pioneered the use of jet boats to navigate on the River Sun Khosi in east Nepal. Jets of compressed water replaced the usual propeller of the motor boat. Jet boats cannot climb rock-strewn rapids without the hazard of hull damage. Even so, considerable progress was made with this first experiment before one of the boats capsized and broke up in a severe rapid.

In 1972, Michel Peissel and David Alexander experimented with single-seat inflatable hovercraft on stretches of a number of Nepali rivers. Having made some progress up part of the lower reaches of the Kali Gandaki, they then lifted their craft by helicopter to Lete above the cataracts and successfully navigated the shallows as far as Marpha. Hovercraft manufacturer Michael Pinder had helped to prepare their craft for this experiment. He subsequently manufactured their lightweight sports craft under the name Skima 1. In addition to our River Rovers, we had purchased an inflatable Skima 4 hovercraft, a direct descendant of the craft used by Peissel. We would have further opportunity to test this on stretches unreached in 1972.

The majority of the river miles chosen for our operation had never previously been navigated. River Rover would be seeking regularly to tackle this fast-flowing rapid-strewn, snow-fed river — carrying up to 1,000 pounds weight of freight. We were about to put our hovercraft's performance and reliability to their severest test yet. River Rover and its launching-site were now ready.

FIVE

MOMENT OF TRUTH

It was a fine, clear day on 18 December 1978 when the River Rover first took to the fast-flowing waters of the Kali Gandaki. For the members of the expedition it was the moment of truth. How would River Rover perform on this treacherous Himalayan river with its whirlpools, undertows, rapids and powerful currents flanked by rock faces?

With a short burst of life, Gerry allowed the craft to slide inch by inch down, down the sandy man-made gap in the rock shelf. Human brakes prevented the craft from leaving the curving path we had prepared. Shouted instructions were totally lost and visibility reduced in our private sandstorm, but frenzied arm-waving sufficed. The note of the craft's Renault engine increased in pitch; gliding along on its cushion of air, the River Rover crept over the last few inches of dry land and swept into the 'fast lane' of the river which gushed out of the Base Camp rapid. The rock wall slid out of view and we made the short trip across the river to our chosen beach.

The sheer power of the water prevented the use of our canoes to recover the crew from the opposite bank. An eventful scramble around the south bank and back to Ramdi bridge brought the day to a close. Our unfamiliarity with the terrain resulted in an expected half-hour return stretching to three hours following the onset of darkness. Next day, local fisherman, Jemman Singh, showed us another route along a precarious path which traversed the riverside cliff. This was admittedly shorter but certainly got the adrenalin flowing!

We returned the compliment by transporting Jemman Singh back across the river by hovercraft. He was the first Nepali ever to travel by hovercraft. Throughout the short journey his face wore a fixed grin, whether of delight or terror we never ascertained.

RAF Stations have a three-fold organization to control flying, engineering and administration. I gave Exercise Kali-Cushion three sections: Operations, Logistics and Base Camp. Captain Gerry Bradman would be responsible for the operations' wing. Working the long supply-line would stretch Flight Lieutenant Paddy Gallacher's skills to the full. Base Camp organization, including radio communications, would be in the hands of advance party leader, Major Dennis Cooper, until the rear party leader Lieutenant Commander Brian Holdsworth arrived. (At this stage, sadly, essential Army duties would call for Dennis to return to the Siberian conditions of the UK.)

Stage 1 of the expedition was planned to last from 18 December 1978 until 1 January, its aim being to establish the handling capabilities of River Rover over a variety of rapids as well as on the fast-water stretches that flush the narrow precipitous gorges. In this period, we also aimed to establish an up-river camp and to select Camp 1 down-river as the site of the first mobile clinic.

Well-satisfied with the evening meal cooked by the Sherpas, the team was beginning to assemble round

the camp fire for the detailed briefing of Stage 1.
Turning down a second helping of ginger pudding, I
slipped away. I wanted a quiet moment to commit
myself to the special challenge of the lonely task of
leadership which would be mine for the next three
and a half months.

Expeditions are rarely short of volunteers. But
fewer are willing to assume the responsibilities of
absolute leadership. My Christian faith was sure to be
put to the test daily, and I asked for strength from God
for all the practical tasks involved. I knew that I would
need to draw on a strength greater than my own.

A sense of expectancy pervaded the briefing. I
emphasized that the times ahead would be especially
testing for those with the support task who would
need to burn themselves out for others, completing
crucial phases of the river journey. The many team
members who readily appreciated this fact were to
provide the backbone of the whole expedition. These
stalwarts were capable of versatility, coupled with the
self-sacrifice which avoids the clamour for obvious
reward.

However good the organization, team members
begin to run down after eight to ten weeks of a tough
expedition. In this phase we would be particularly
accident-prone. Endurance, determination, flexibility
and loyalty would be constant requirements. Mine
was the task of creating a depth of team spirit as a
reservoir to be drawn on in times of stress and strain.

The briefing over, we sat round the fire fanning the
smoke away from our faces and contemplating the
future encounter with the furies of the Kali Gandaki.
The tumbling waters of the Base Camp rapid and the
calm of the bankside pools acted as a reminder of the
unique blend of excitement and tranquility which the
river had in store.

For the next six days we rarely ventured more than
ten miles from base as we tested the craft on a series of

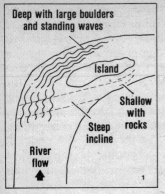

Deep with large boulders and standing waves

Island

Shallow with rocks

Steep incline

River flow

1

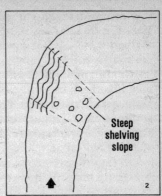

Steep shelving slope

2

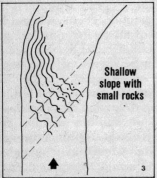

Shallow slope with small rocks

3

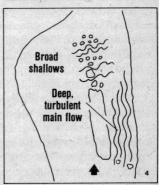

Broad shallows

Deep, turbulent main flow

4

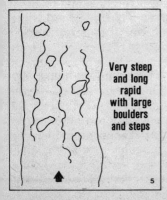

Very steep and long rapid with large boulders and steps

5

Pilot Gerry Bradnam identified five main types of rapid. It was often easier to take River Rover up these rapids than to come back down them.

typical Himalayan rapids down-river. Each obstacle had its own characteristics. The river had few straight stretches, following a winding course of tight bends for many miles.

Gerry developed a technique similar to that employed by car rally drivers — pulling out to the outer bank before the bend and passing close to the inner bank at the apex of the bend. Speed before entry was kept low and power increased on the commencement of the turn.

As confidence grew, more complicated rapids were tackled. Once the hovercraft was in the white water descending a rapid, it gathered momentum and it was essential to lose excess speed in order to maintain full control before it began to reel on the crests of broken water. The drivers cultivated an ability to 'read' a rapid. Prior assessment is essential if the pilot is to keep ahead of events, rather than merely reacting to circumstances as they arise.

Heading along a short straight in the river, we build up speed easily but the roar of billowing waters ahead sends out a warning. From the sublime serenity of thirty-four knots, the craft is about to plunge into a boulder-strewn chute of white water. Waves envelop the River Rover. Gerry peers through the spray of the rapid ahead. A moment of sheer terror — and the craft is under control. Next time we will try to land ahead and inspect and pick a line but this is not always possible. River Rover's control system is already proving its worth.

Visibility of the rapid was easier travelling upstream where the main problem was caused by the walls of the gorge enclosing the river. Once again the control system was vital in selecting the route up the rapid alongside the jagged rocks on one side, and avoiding the tumbling white water containing small waterfalls on the other.

Sometimes the only route was through the centre of

rough, kicking water. Early correction on the controls was essential, then power was fully applied to carve out a clearly-intended route up-river. If left too late, the only course would be to turn downstream — often in considerable danger of being swept onto the rocks. Fighting on up-river was often easier than plunging back down the same rapid. Gerry was quickly developing techniques for driving both up and down the various different types of rapid encountered. After three days of operation, he announced, 'A hovercraft with conventional controls wouldn't have lasted five minutes on the Kali Gandaki!'

Our small inflatable Skima 4 hovercraft was successfully launched and operated as a training vehicle on the calmer stretches of the river near Base Camp. In the early stages, we had difficulty in keeping Skima's three two-stroke engines going at the same time. We experienced frequent frights as the more enthusiastic Skima operators strayed unintentionally towards difficult rapids, seemingly forgetting that this hovercraft does not have brakes!

The bankside at Base Camp quickly became an open attraction for the villagers of Ramdighat and also for hundreds of Nepalese from the surrounding area. They had heard that a bunch of white men had a strange boat that could charge out of the water on to dry land. The village holy man sought me out and requested that River Rover make a special visit to the beach below his rock-hewn temple. It was a matter of prestige for him. The 'Vicarage Lawn', as we called it, became a convenient stopping-point for our regular up-river operations.

The holy man came to our doctors for some medicine — a signal victory we felt. We were less happy — and most puzzled — when one of our British Gurkha corporals developed backache and went for a cure, not to one of our fully-qualified doctors, but to the holy man in his temple.

Despite the relatively higher standard of living of expedition members at Base Camp (even under field conditions), a most cordial rapport developed with the villagers. They gratefully gathered our empty food tins. In the months ahead, nothing was stolen from Base Camp — a fine testimony when the temptation must have been very strong.

The Nepali spectators were joined by an endless parade of wildlife: a hundred birds rising as one from the rock face and swooping across the gorge; a family of monkeys drinking at the water's edge and then bounding up the steeply shelving bank, disturbed by the unexpected arrival of our craft.

A boulder-strewn beach 150 yards downstream from Base Camp would be well suited as a landing site for River Rover once the rock debris had been removed. Villagers were pleased to do this demolition work, being more than satisfied with the 10 rupees (40p) per day they would be paid for the job.

While the rock removers beavered away, young Nepali boys bathed naked in the nearby pools. Two of these lads wore the sacred thread (janai) over their shoulders, marking them out as high-caste Brahmins, the priestly sect. The others belonged to the lower artisan caste: carpenters, stonemasons, goldsmiths, or the porters on whose backs huge loads are painstakingly carried over Nepal's tortuous terrain for a smaller daily wage than we paid to our friendly rock-breakers.

The Nepalis accept their status passively and look to reincarnation to improve their lot. It is only as a result of virtuous deeds that they can expect to be reborn at a higher level; bad deeds will send them into some lower caste or, even worse, will cause them to return as an animal or insect. Thus the artisan is resigned to his position. Any misfortune is seen as the consequence of a foolish act in a former life. For the Nepali, religion is

Nepali children were fascinated by the expedition and its equipment – even by pilot Gerry Bradnam's improvised fly-swat!

an obstacle to improving the quality of life. No questions are asked.

Early on Christmas Eve, we hovered River Rover across the rock shallows and ventured up-river for the first time. After a brief pause on the Vicarage Lawn at the mouth of the gorge, River Rover set out to tackle the furies of a staircase of rapids which punctuate the immediate up-river area. Gerry gave himself and his crew a nerve-testing ride upstream. This run was very likely the most challenging ever undertaken by a light-weight hovercraft to date.

After the first six-mile return journey, Gerry returned looking noticeably pale. His confidence grew on the second attempt. As his front-seat crew on this second run, I experienced a nerve-racking first ride. One 250-yard uphill stretch of boiling water consisted of a succession of standing waves. Manoeuvring around the worst obstacles the craft battled upstream, at times almost enveloped in the cascading water.

Steering was becoming a true art form, made possible only by the craft's unique control system. Enclosed within box structures behind the propulsion fans are the two horizontal control surfaces known as elevons. Moving elevons in opposite senses causes the craft to bank into a turn. This system gives far better directional stability than any hovercraft have ever previously achieved. Anyone could have thought of it, one observer remarked before we left Britain.

It was Tim Longley's simple spark of genius which made our expedition possible. Gerry's driving skills were already making full use of the potential of Tim's invention, and as our thoughts turned to Christmas, we realized that the upstream aspects would test both team and machines to the limits.

It was 25 December — just one week after River Rover's first encounter with the Kali Gandaki. I was up before daybreak on Christmas morning. Dawn broke in the time it took to drink a mug of well-brewed tea. Our simple Communion service used tinned fruit juice in place of the wine and Army hard tack as a substitute for the bread. My thoughts turned to home as, enjoying the long shadows cast by the early morning sun, I sat by the deep-green waters of the Kali Gandaki to open the present from my family which had been lovingly prepared way back in November.

We had bought a supply of games, sweets and balloons for the children of the village. As we climbed the hill-top, we saw that the whole school had assembled to greet us. The orderly queue of youngsters quickly changed to a seething mass of upturned hands as we sought to give out the goodies. As we left after tea with the elders, garlanded with wild flowers, the village headman asked me to be the guest of honour at their celebrations of the King of Nepal's official birthday, to be held four days later on 29 December.

Back at base, Donald Bruce had prepared a home-from-home Christmas lunch thanks to the Navy's victuallers who had painstakingly packed the festive foodstuffs, and also included a welcome card of Christmas greetings.

Even on Christmas Day the stimulating challenge of the river was never far from our thoughts. The plunging water of the rapid at Base Camp provided us with an ever-present reminder of the dangers. We had already seen the bodies of two Nepalis, swept away and drowned while carrying out their ritual ablutions.

This memorable day concluded with a visit to the United Mission Hospital at Tansen, described by Peter Dixon:

'The end of our compo ration Christmas lunch was by no means the end of our Christmas Day activities. After the food had settled, the majority of the team piled into our dilapidated Mercedes minibus and set out on the twisting road to Tansen, accepting the invitation of the mission hospital to share in their Christmas evening celebrations. Like Christians all over the world, the missionaries in Nepal have their own particular way of celebrating Christmas, one of the two major events of the Christian calendar. Missionaries from all over the Palpa district — doctors, nurses, agriculturists and engineers — had travelled to Tansen, mostly on foot, to spend Christmas Day together.

'Shortly before the minibus reached the town of Tansen, we disembarked to take the short cut up the steep hill to the hospital. Panting towards the top of the hill, we started to wonder if we were losing our sanity. We thought we could hear the incongruous strains of bagpipes drifting down the hill. As we neared the hospital, the figure of a lone piper appeared by the walls. A Scottish medical student, doing voluntary service at Tansen, had brought his bagpipes with him, as others might bring a guitar or harmonica.

'The idea of a piper at Tansen seemed preposterous, and yet at the same time peculiarly appropriate, for Tansen Mission Hospital has something of the fortress about it. It stands on a hill, alone but for a small village of *bhattis* (tea-houses) which has grown up to serve, or perhaps to fleece, patients' relatives who need food and shelter.

'The isolated site was the only plot of ground the government would allow the mission to use, mainly because the Nepalis thought that it was haunted by evil spirits and plagued by jackals. The hospital compound itself is a forbidding sight, fenced and walled all around. Some of us felt that this seemed inappropriate for a hospital run by missionaries, but the explanation given by the staff was simple. There were many young Nepali girls living in the compound being trained as nurses, and their parents had to be convinced of their daughters' security before letting them leave home.

'The form of the "Christmas party" seemed strange to some of the team members who went to Tansen, but for me it came a close second to being at home with my family. The nurses gave us a Nepali cap for each team member. This is tightly worn and flower-pot shaped, and is one of the symbols of Nepal. I was told that the origin of the cap is in the shape of a Himalayan peak — as likely as explanation as any, I suppose! There was more food, of course — a cold buffet provided by the mission families living at Tansen. We were amazed at how resourceful they were with the limited foodstuffs available.

'But most of the evening was devoted to a celebration of the birth of Christ. About fifty of us crowded into the living-room of one of the doctors, sitting cross-legged on the floor and filling every available inch of space. We sang joyful carols and spent time in prayer, and read the first chapter of John's Gospel: "And the Word became flesh and dwelt among us, full of grace and truth." A group of the hospital staff performed part of Dorothy L. Sayer's play *The Man Born to be King*, adding further meaning to our gathering.

'But the most satisfying feature of the day was the privilege of sharing the celebration with a group of people who had given up much of what we take for granted, in order to serve God. All in all, a true "family Christmas" 6,000 miles from home.'

We now set out to operate the craft to the limit on the most testing of the rapids to the north and west of Ramdighat, all of which were graded as severe. The water level had fallen noticeably even during the short period we had spent at base. Each rainless day increased the severity of the more difficult rapids. As the water level dropped, rock beds were uncovered, causing the main river flow to become narrower and more turbulent and more difficult to navigate. We did engage in some 'local modifications' to clear a channel through some shallows.

Kit stowed, life jackets adjusted, cabin closed —

we're ready to go. Increasing the engine power, we glide easily down the sandy slipway of the Vicarage Lawn, hover momentarily on the shallows, and then move off down-river into the deep water. Moving across to one side of the river, we find an area wide enough to turn in. Slowing the River Rover down, the elevons are applied and she heads round. Increasing the power, we line up against the current sweeping towards us. A fine spray as full power is applied as we seek to climb over hump. Reading eighteen knots, we reduce power. Noticeably spray-free, we keep to the centre of the river as we head up the gorge, concentrating fiercely on the lookout for rapids ahead.

'Going over hump' is similar to planing in a sailing dinghy. The 'hump' is the wave of water created by the air escaping under the skirt of the craft. The downward thrust of air which lifts the craft creates a hollow depression in the water. As speed increases, this hole in the water under the craft moves forward and produces waves. Increased speed enables the craft to climb on top of its bow wave and it begins to plane. The drag is decreased and the craft goes faster, even when throttled back. Since water is over 800 times denser than air, the mechanical advantage of our hovercraft over a boat is most noticeable once hump has been surmounted. (Appendix B describes this more fully.)

The exhilaration at the controls of River Rover at thirty knots, pushing aside the efforts of the current of a giant Himalayan river, gives a fleeting feeling of mastery which is soon dispelled by a maze of partially-submerged rocks ahead — fortunately well 'sign-posted' by large standing waves.

We quickly reach the first large rapid, on both sides of which are sheer rock faces. The white water surging across the shallows is split in two by a small island. One side is deeper, the other barely awash. Keeping the nose into the tongue of white water, we head for the deeper right-hand side. The foaming water is peppered with small rocks. Applying full power we surge forward from crest to crest. As we reach the top of the climb we are forced towards the left. A flip on the elevon brings us back on course. We are gaining speed as we surge through the centre of a violent flow and emerge into the thin ripple of fast-flowing water at the top of the chute we have just climbed.

The morning sun has now burned away the last of the river mist giving a clear view of the obstacles ahead. The walls of the gorge seem closer and the sun has yet to penetrate into the deeper recesses of this section of the river. The rapid ahead has been artificially funnelled by a large fish trap built across the ideal forward path for the hovercraft. We're surprised, as the ragged line of wooden stakes has been put there since our initial foray two days earlier. Our surprise is mild compared with the look on the faces of the fishermen as we approach!

There's a boiling cauldron of white water ahead with the full force of the river foaming against a towering rock wall. Gerry lines the craft up, avoiding both the swirling waters to the right and the spears of the fish trap to the left. We use full power against the slope and the strength of the river eternally fed by the snows of the world's greatest mountain range. We battle with the fast turbulent flow, plunging from crest to crest.

Finally, with some relief, we reach the top and head gratefully into a tranquil pool above this torrent. Gerry wipes his brow, elated at the progress, but is clearly fatigued by the battle against the thrust of these unknown rapids. Looking back we're unable to see the start of this rapid because of the steepness of the gradient. (This obstacle was to become a favourite site for the BBC camera team and provided the spectacular opening sequence when the film was subsequently screened.)

A brief pause and we carry on up-river, a sheer rock wall to our right and densely forested slopes to the left. The rivers in Nepal, in common with the country's few roads, are frequently resculptured by surprise land-slips. Ahead of us, a huge mound of rock debris had been deposited in the centre of the river. To one side of it, the main flow poured like milk from a giant churn turned on its side. On the other side, a shallow twisting stream tunnelled deeply into the rim of the rock mound.

We park River Rover on a convenient sand spit at the front of the rock mound and set about investigat-ing a route through. Which side should we attempt? The stream was barely wide enough for River Rover, whereas the milky torrent posed a threat to both the craft and its occupants. We often had to tread this fine line between purposeful adventure and unnecessary risk in pioneering a new technique on this, one of the most violent rivers in the world.

We explore the narrow stream chiselled through the rock debris. It might just be possible for River Rover to hover between the large boulders deposited by the undermining work of the raging waters of a previous monsoon. Gerry edges the craft gently into the bubbling waters at the entrance to the stream. The groove in the debris goes progressively deeper. With great care the craft is eased between two sentinel rocks threatening like giant nut crackers to crush the elevon boxes. River Rover is thrust irreversibly forward; the only way out is to traverse the obstacles. Ahead the stream bubbles over a series of rocky ridges and a sloping sandbank. The flexibility of River Rover's skirt enables the brush with the abrasive objects in the gully to be absorbed by the yielding rubber fabric.

The way forward to the rear of the rock mound requires a climb rising to one in nine, equivalent to low gear engagement on an ordinary road. Increasing power, River Rover emerges with some relief at the

**Pilot Peter Dixon finds that total concentration is
called for when handling the craft.**

top of the staircase. The craft has tackled a narrow, steep-sided gully littered with obstacles and has emerged unscathed. Although less spectacular than the climbs on the white water rapids, the technical significance of this achievement is to have equal impact for the aims of the expedition.

The arrival of River Rover has disturbed two vultures tearing at an indistinguishable piece of flesh, probably human, left high and dry on a sandy inlet by a flash flood. They climb quickly away and then glide high above us, their giant wings beating in slow but powerful time, as they watch and wait for our departure before swooping down to the carcass again. Alas, this was to be a frequent encounter: the poorer folk are often unable to afford enough firewood to complete a cremation properly, and the ravages of the river and the vultures complete the task. We became so familiar with this startling riverside scene that we ceased to be shocked.

Pleased with progress, we decide to retrace our steps to Ramdighat, well aware that descending the rapids we had climbed would call for a different but equally skilled adroitness of hand and eye by Gerry. We approach the lip of each rapid at low speed with the bow up, in order to maintain full hover height against the protruding rocks. Speed picks up as the craft bucks on the standing waves of the steeply descending staircase. Gerry is closely monitoring speed, making sure that full manoeuvrability is maintained to enable a sure path down the high-velocity water chutes. Safely through the difficult fish-trap rapid, I catch a glimpse of a cluster of thatched, wooden-framed houses precariously perched on the crest of the lofty slope. The veranda on each house is prominent even from a distance. (It is not possible for anyone of a different caste to eat in a strict Hindu house, so hospitality must take place on the veranda.)

It takes us just twenty minutes to cover the seven

miles back to the Vicarage Lawn. At Base Camp, Peter Hitchin — in charge of the Leprosy Control Programme based at the Shining Hospital in Pokhara — has called en route for a well-deserved holiday in India. Peter is responsible for pioneering this work in the far west of Nepal. I gave him a spin in Skima 4 to whet his appetite for hovercraft operations.

Petrol was the lifeblood of our project, for without adequate supplies, the hovercraft operations would quickly come to a halt. With this in mind, we planned to maintain a reserve holding of 200 gallons over and above our estimated weekly consumption of ninety gallons at the peak of operations, to fuel two River Rovers, Skima 4 and Gemini.

The crisis in Iran was already making fuel supplies unpredictable. Although we had a special permit, obtaining fuel was frequently complicated by minor officials who insisted that we renew our dispensation or seek special clearance from the district officer. However, on the two occasions I made the fuel run to Pokhara, I obtained as much as I wanted with no hassle. Such were the variations and uncertainties. The fuel was always of poor quality (less than ninety octane) and this caused pre-ignition in the engines. Water contamination was so persistent that we filtered all stock through chamois — just one of the many innovations suggested by our resourceful REME sergeant, Rick Elliott, before we left the UK.

On one occasion, Paddy managed to purchase 150 gallons of high octane aviation fuel at Kathmandu Airport, which, when blended with our 'Pokhara 90', produced a very usable mixture. The fuel negotiations at Pokhara were often protracted, necessitating an overnight stay. The mission folk at the Shining Hospital provided us with excellent hospitality and we were able to probe their extensive knowledge of local customs.

These trips to Pokhara gave some light relief to our minibus driver Ramansigh and his youthful assistant Hari. Ramansigh spent an inordinate amount of time in the track-side *bhattis*, where the young women seemed to find his big trucker image appealing. On one occasion, Hari came to the Shining Hospital as Dennis Cooper and Paddy were at breakfast. He was clearly agitated and, gesticulating furiously, indicated that Ram was in some sort of trouble. They couldn't understand exactly what the trouble was, but when Hari cut the air above his head with an imaginary sword, Paddy speculated that our driver had been given a summary execution by an irate father brandishing a *kukri*.

They followed Hari to a village on the outskirts of town. Ram was in a prison cell. As he drove into the village the previous evening, his bus had collided with some overhead cables which were supporting the wall of a house. Unfortunately, the house owner was the local *mukia* (headman), who had promptly impounded the bus and held Ram in custody until suitable compensation was provided. Fuel runs to Pokhara were always eventful!

We planned that River Rover would make two 'round-trip' journeys to the 'White House', as we called our up-river site. From a vantage-point 2,000 feet above the Kali Gandaki, I had viewed the course of the river upstream of the furthest point reached so far. Almost four miles further on, the river turned through a sharp loop, at the mouth of which a fearful torrent plunged through a funnel between two boulder-fields. Aware of the magnitude of this obstruction, I planned a two-day up-river trip with an overnight camp at the nearest convenient site to the giant rapid. A self-contained trekking party would closely follow the twisting trail, both to observe River Rover in action and to experience at firsthand the laborious trek.

At 7.30 a.m., after a full English breakfast and with

the riverside mist beginning to disperse, the trekking group set out on the journey to the White House — ten miles by river, nearer sixteen on foot. Trekking in Nepal has its own special feeling. Throughout the day, the sound of running water never left our ears, which were always straining for the high pitched note of River Rover's ducted fans. 'Namaste, namaste': a group of shyly smiling youngsters, unsure of our strange white faces, met us on the trail, folding their hands together above their chests in the traditional Nepalese greeting. We responded in like manner.

We were fascinated by the variety of the terrain and by a people whose way of life is still largely untouched by the West. At 10 a.m. we paused for a snack. This is the time of day when Nepalis take their main meal. Ingeniously, the Army caterers had produced tinned *daalbaat* for Gurkhas Purnasing and Shovaram. For the riverside dweller, this meal would consist of a quantity of rice with a thin lentil soup to pour over it; occasionally some cooked vegetables, or a little meat (*daal*) is added. Purna and Shov tucked into their traditional Nepali meal made hardly recognizable by the accompanying liberal quantities of Army meat and vegetables.

The trail frequently leaves the riverside, and a steep climb ensues to link the isolated houses clustered at irregular intervals high on the slope of the gorge. Inevitably the pathway routes back down nearly 2,000 feet to the river again. Avoiding one climb down, we took a short cut across a line of dry paddy terraces to the village of Darpuk which I had viewed yesterday from the river. Or was it Darpuk? I asked Purna to check. He asked three or four villagers, and was given three or four different answers. 'How far to the river loop?' I asked, forgetting that distance is measured in days rather than miles. The villagers are natural, friendly and as helpful as they can be. They have no reason to know the name of even one of the great snowy peaks they view each day. The mountains make life so hard and their ambition may well be to follow the well-trodden route to the Terai, where the land is flat and easy to work.

By the time we reached the planned rendezvous at the seven-mile rock slip, River Rover was sitting primly on the sand spit whilst the crew of Gerry, Bruce Vincent and Peter Dixon were sunning themselves. Having left base at 10.15 a.m., they had completed two return journeys with time to spare. On the second run, River Rover had covered the seven miles in just twenty-two minutes — we had been on trek for three and a half hours.

Peter was earmarked as the principal driver of Rover 02, due to arrive in Nepal at the end of January. Gerry was already able to pass on to Peter the valuable lessons he had learnt. Whilst Gerry could never relax on this fast-flowing river, he was beginning to map out a regular pathway up and down the staircase of hazardous rapids. Danger is ever-present: if the engine should cut or the hull of the craft below the skirt be splintered on a rock protruding higher than fourteen inches (i.e. above the hover height), the crew would be at the mercy of the Kali Gandaki and its white water, whirlpools and undertows. The crew wear partially-inflated life jackets and the craft would float following power failure; nevertheless, the worst of the turbulent rapids in this forge section had, I was certain, power to crush our craft. The possibility of accident was to be graphically illustrated next day by Gemini.

The trekking party waited long enough to witness a repeat of River Rover's notable climb round the rock mound, then continued up the gorge. The river flow grew in volume and the speed of the waves on the rapids increased into heavy chops and swirls. Even the water close to the bank gurgled and sucked. Three miles upstream we saw a small white-washed cottage on the far side of the river above a large boulder-field.

We selected a nearside camp site on a sandy ridge, liberally supplied with driftwood. The broader sweep of the river just here provided us with both camp site and launching-point. Ahead the scenery was impressive, the gorge narrowing until the cliffs tower on either side. River Rover glided on to the sandbank and as the engine died, the craft gently settled like a duck nestling down on its eggs. The roar of the tumultuous rapid about half a mile up-river upset an otherwise peaceful setting.

We walked across several small tributaries on convenient bridges formed by bleached tree trunks, their tenuous hold on the steep slopes having been undermined in a previous monsoon. Clambering over slippery rocks, mossy logs and twisted roots, we hoisted ourselves up on to a rocky promontory at the side of the rapid, close enough to feel the thin wisps of residual spray from the crest of the waves. In front of us were 300 yards of white water surging steeply down through rock walls. The run was littered with sizeable boulders, sweeping the white water into large waves with curling tops. From yesterday's long-range viewpoint, I might have minimized the dangers involved in tackling the crashing force of this obstacle; standing by this monster, we now had to shout to be heard.

While I was busy looking for a route through the boulder-field using the craft's amphibious capabilities, Gerry and Peter agreed to take River Rover for an exploratory nibble at the base of the rapid. We recorded Gerry's remarks as he was driving:

'This is the most difficult stretch of water I've ever experienced — in any hovercraft. The concentration necessary is terrific. You can't afford to relax for a second. I've driven the standard SRN6 with my Army squadron, which is of course much larger than River Rover and you feel safer, you are higher up and have more metal around you. But I don't think the SRN6 would have been able to operate on this particular river — not on rapids of this size. I don't think they have the manoeuvrability of this little craft. When you consider that we're able to steer up these very steep rapids, that's really something!' (Gerry voices his feelings as he approaches the rapid.) 'This rapid must be 350 yards long and it's white water the whole width of the river. And I — I don't think we shall be able to make this one to the top, I'm trying — trying to get up between the rock wall and the worst of the white water here — but it's getting very turbulent — we'll barely make it. We are going to have to go down backwards. Hold on. Hold on — we're going on to the rocks.' (At this point, Gerry used all his skill to turn the craft broadside to the current and make his escape, heading thankfully down the rapid, easing away from the powerful current which was snatching the craft towards the rocks.)

'Now we're going to stop and have another look at this one. That was really bad — a real pig. We got about halfway up but just couldn't make the rest. And I noticed that as we got nearer the top, the large waves enveloped the craft.' (Although in theory, River Rover has no contact with the water surface, in practice the drag of water does slow the craft down in the most turbulent rapids.)

'One of the dangers is that if you get picked up by a big wave, there's a real possibility that you'll be dropped on to one of those boulders. Well, that's it in this gorge, unless we can get across the boulder-field.'

We knew that for a distance of two miles up-river we faced about six of the most formidable obstacles on the whole of the Kali Gandaki, resulting from the determined effort of the river to break out of the Mahabharat at this point and take the shortest route to the plains. From my trekking observations in 1975, I knew that the stretch further to the north and west and as far as Baglung would be fully navigable by River

Crowds of colourful Nepalis appear wherever the
craft beaches. And Tony Maher always manages to
keep them amused.

Rover once we had penetrated this two-mile blockade.

The gorge filled with shadows and dusk fell in the time it took to make a camp fire with the liberal supply of stranded driftwood. A crowd of Nepalis appeared within minutes and then stood for hours staring at our strange habits. Food from tins was particularly puzzling. The 'Eastern stare' is initially a disconcerting habit, but one soon realizes that our ideas about privacy and rudeness are purely part of our Western culture. Later, a line of blazing torches appeared at the river's edge. The patient, loincloth-clad fishermen, whose way of life has not changed for centuries, use these lights to attract the large mahseer fish towards their traps. As we drank our night cap, the torches approached our camp site and these friendly fisherfolk squatted on their haunches round our fire to thaw out their limbs frozen from hours of paddling in the raw, ice-fed waters.

The 'Gemini', a five-section inflatable boat, with wooden transom and dock planking and a semi-rigid keel, is used by the Royal Marines for landing troops in coastal areas and estuaries. For its weight (350 pounds), it has a large carrying capacity; its stability, speed, high buoyancy and shallow draught are major advantages.

In the early stages of the expedition, our Gemini was used for reconnaissance up-river from Base Camp; it was able to operate in both directions on limited deep-water sections and would be used for supply carrying for down-river operations. For these, the engine would be stowed on board so that the in-water power source did not restrict its progress, and the craft would become an inflatable paddle-steered raft. If necessary, Gemini could be deflated and be transported back to base in the hold of River Rover.

Tony Maher, our tough Marine with the soft heart, was determined to take Gemini to the limit. The same man who would head his craft fearlessly down a rock-strewn torrent was also a natural attraction for the Nepali village children. His improvised games quickly established our acceptance on even the loneliest beach. His ready smile and sense of fun has that special quality which is so infectious to children the world over.

I had agreed, with a little persuasion, that Tony, together with Ben Bennett, Dave Porter and Robin Dugdale, could go up-river in Gemini, provided that they carried the craft round the worst rapids. On the day of their trip, there were four empty places at supper — Tony and Gemini were overdue. With the meal over and plans for a search and rescue already forming in my mind, four soaked and chilled crew squelched into base.

Tony related what had happened:

'We made excellent up-river time to the rapid above the rock mound. Our portage had improved with each obstacle. I decided to turn for base.' (Hurtling down the rapids is an exhilarating encounter — and an experience Tony couldn't resist.) 'Life-jackets inflated, crash-hats adjusted, we checked the lashings which held the waterproof equipment bags to the gunwhales. We headed for the sizeable rapid between the towering rock conglomerates. With the engine stowed, Ben and I paddled to keep the craft straight. Dave and Robin hung on tight, ready to throw their weight in the best direction.

'The flow of water quickened and we bounced from crest to crest. Halfway down we cannoned off a submerged rock. Paddle right, paddle left — then we were too far to the left and were sucked towards a stopper wave. Gemini's bow was lifted at least ten feet in the air. At the same time, another creaming current hit us broadside on and over we went. We fought to hang on to Gemini, but the force of the water prized open our tenuous hold and jettisoned us into the main surge of the rapid. We lost each other completely as the swirling water and undercurrents took control.

'I fought to the surface and took a deep breath, before being bowled over by the current. Taking gulps of air when I could and swimming as hard as possible, I managed to edge out of the main flow into an eddy. I looked around anxiously, blowing water out of my mouth and nose, and was relieved to see three other bedraggled figures. Watery smiles of relief all round! Heavy bruising apart we were intact — but there was no sign of Gemini.

'About half a mile downstream a hard rock outcrop jutted into the main current. Wedged between this outcrop and a partially-submerged rock, washed by a violent flow of passing water, was our upturned Gemini. Wading thigh-deep in icy water trying to untangle safety lines with numbed fingers whilst preventing the craft from running free again, proved a testing exercise for the crew. Four of the waterproof bags had been torn from their moorings, but the thick rubber skin had taken its punishment well. The outboard motor was intact but two of the paddles had been splintered!'

With improvised paddles, Tony and his crew circumspectly returned to base.

But Tony's spirit is not easily dampened. He was already organizing the village children to search for the missing bags offering rewards of sweets! But the capsize incident had emphasized the difficulty of operating the craft on the variety of water found on the Kali Gandaki. Shallow water, more than anything else, slowed Gemini down — and some lengths of the river had fast-flowing water that was as little as three inches deep. In these conditions, where the River Rover was in its element, the Gemini crew would have to use paddles — and use them quickly and expertly!

In the event, the Johnson outboard engine performed extremely well: its dependability and ease of starting saving the occupants from many potentially dangerous situations. By the end of the expedition, the boat itself had suffered one puncture to the hull, several lost decking hinges and two broken keel pieces. This was far less damage than was to be expected, considering the severe conditions in which the Gemini was used.

29 December was an eventful day. In the evening, four of us climbed to the hill-top village of Malunga to take part in the king's birthday celebrations.

Eight rough-hewn, wooden chairs had been placed outside the school house facing down the slope towards a very temporary outdoor stage. This was flanked on either side by curtains, delicately embroidered with a coiled cobra pattern, and clearly kept for such auspicious occasions. I was given the central seat of honour, flanked by members of the village *Panchayat* (local council) and the Brahmin priests. The whole village squatted in a densely packed mass around us. I could barely move my feet.

After several false starts, the festivities began with the playing of large horns and a variety of flutes. This was interspersed with pleasing drumming undertaken with the tips of the fingers on a double-ended drum. The repetitive, pulsating rhythm set the audience swaying. The prolonged programme consisted of songs, tale-telling, riddles and dancing in which young men impersonated girls. Unscheduled interludes extended the marathon performance, as the two ancient tilley lamps providing the stage lighting needed frequent pumping.

As the excitement level rose, the villagers crowded towards the stage. The marshals kept order by indiscriminately clubbing the heads of the over-enthusiastic with a short, thick stick. This drastic admonition was accepted passively and with resignation by the recipients, and with much mirth by those who had kept their distance.

After three hours in the seat of honour and with the

music still going strong, I was escorted to the school house to have a meal with the headman — liberal helpings of rice, mutton and vegetables washed down with hot, steaming tea. Purna informed me that the headman wanted some of his young men to join the British Gurkhas. This is one political subject I wished to avoid, so I politely replied that I belonged to the Air Force! As an act of friendship, I made a donation to the Malunga school extension fund on behalf of the expedition.

The balance of the team had attended more in-formal celebrations back at Ramdighat, and I had been asleep for an hour or so when Paddy returned from fulfilling his cultural obligations. I vaguely remember him struggling to get his socks off. I stirred some two hours later and he was still trying to solve his sock problem. The celebration village rum called *rakshi* had a fiery potency which had taken Paddy by surprise!

THE SCOPE OF THE PROBLEM

'Auspicious' has a special meaning in Nepal. His Majesty King Birenda delayed his coronation for three years because in January 1972 he was 30 and the Nepali year was 2030. The '0' was inauspicious.

The Tuesday of each week is considered an unlucky day to start a journey or a new course of action. Auspicious or not, Tuesday 1 January 1979 was a significant day for Exercise Kali-Cushion. We were ready for operations in earnest. Bearing in mind Kipling's warning about the early grave awaiting those who try to change the East, we now set about tackling the expedition's goal: to explore the seventy-five miles of the mysterious Kali Gandaki as it flowed west to east along the northern flank of the Mahabharat Lekh range, seeking to escape into the plains of the Terai. Sixty of these miles concided with the boundary of the Palpa rural health scheme, ten miles above Base Camp and fifty below. To be able to navigate both ways between the bridge at Ramdighat and the ferry crossing at Narayanghat would forge a life-saving communication link.

We had learnt valuable operating lessons up-river.

Although each rapid was different from the next, we were developing an art for negotiating the five main types of rapid encountered (see diagram in chapter 5). The rapids down-river to the east would be challenging if a little less perilous than the treacherous barriers which stood up-river. We were now to test River Rover in relation to the specific practical task for which it had been designed. Nine miles down-river Gerry found a suitable location for Camp 1, to be the site of our first mobile clinic.

We had come a long way. Now was the moment of opportunity. As the expedition leader, I was fired by a process of possibility thinking which could only see the project progressing to a successful conclusion. Ignoring the possibility of defeat, I was ready to plunge into this riverside manifestation of an unjust world with all the strength I could muster. All very heady stuff, the prudence of which was certainly questioned from time to time by the more pragmatic members of the team. Repeatedly treating seeming setbacks as positive progress and refusing to accept adverse circumstances as anything but a providential change of plan can be wearing for a military team trained to react to the practical realities of any given task.

From the outset, many of the team shared the visionary nature of my approach, while others needed to be convinced. Paddy Gallacher and Peter Dixon were to provide an effective brake on any excess that might result from such a vehement pursuit of the goal. I shared a tent at base and a close bond of fellowship with Paddy. He wore his emotions on his sleeve and he also took the feelings of team members very much to heart. This was a useful and ever-present barometer to me.

Peter, outwardly unexcitable, cool and collected, nevertheless had a deep commitment to the project. He had the special gift of tuning into the consensus, thus ensuring that I drew on the combined experience of

On smooth stretches, the craft reached speeds of
thirty-four knots with virtually no spray.

the team. In this way Peter made a notable contribution to the unity of the project.

Formal briefings were kept short, discussion confined to the facts and the plans for the next phase of actions. I attempted to get my ideas across through informal chats with team members. I was absolutely convinced of one thing: the ultimate objective of the expedition was entirely valid and worthwhile. If we succeeded, we would have shown that a hovercraft service on a previously unnavigable river could make a valuable contribution to the communication system and health care of a remote area in a desperately needy underdeveloped country.

As I thought once again of River Rover's potential, I remembered Bill Gould's descriptions of the sort of hazardous journeys that missionaries in Nepal have to be prepared to undertake:

'Frequently we at home take our journeys for granted. We often embark on a 200-mile journey by car without even committing the journey to God. But our missionary friends overseas are constantly exposed to dangers and difficulties and a prayer for them for "journeying mercies" is a vital necessity.

'We lived and worked in an area where travel was particularly hazardous and difficult. When we first arrived in Nepal, we used those stalwarts of the second World War — the DC3s. By this time, of course, they were a little the worse for wear: take-off and landing were particularly shattering. The preliminary revving of the engines prior to take-off gave the impression that a force 9 gale was blowing and the whole plane rocked on its foundations. How many times did we pray for a safe journey and how many times did we praise the Lord for answering those prayers!

'But it wasn't only the planes! Travel on buses designed to seat forty people maximum carrying over a hundred either inside or on the roof was also a challenge, particularly as the roads usually curved round one mountain side after another. Travel sickness was common, and I suspect that part of the cause was fear as well as the motion.

'However difficult and frightening the planes and buses were, they were nothing in comparison with river journeys. These took all one's courage. The Nepalis themselves are frightened of their rivers and you can understand this when you see their basic boat design. It is simplicity itself: a tree trunk with a portion gouged out to allow people to crouch in it. Perhaps the most frightening characteristic is its high centre of gravity. Unless everyone on board is crouching as low as possible, the whole thing is unstable. Capsizes are common. Reaching the other side of a fast-flowing river in one of these dug-out ferries is a cause of great rejoicing, not to mention the release of nervous tension!

'Perhaps my most interesting river journey was in the days before we had buses and Land Rovers on the one major road in our region, which was then under construction. We had obtained a German motor cycle to speed up journeys which were normally done on foot. However, in the twenty-six mile journey there was a fast-flowing river to negotiate, but no dug-out ferries and no bridge. For a small fee a man was willing to guide you through the swirling waters which were above waist level. But what could we do with the motor bike? Half a dozen Nepali porters offered to hold this above their heads as they negotiated the waters. Dependable as ever, the Nepalis reached the other side of the river and I continued my journey.

'On another occasion, I had driven from the hospital down through the mountains for about twenty miles when I reached this same river. There was absolutely no way of taking the vehicle across. With the river swollen by monsoon rains, engineers had slung two wire cables across the river, one above the other, separated by an average distance of four feet.

However, at the beginning and end, the distances were considerably wider than that and the cables were tied tightly to concrete supports on either bank. The theory was that you could cross the river without any real problem if you gripped the upper cable with your hands and walked sideways on the lower cable. The whole exercise was a shade incongruous because at the starting-point one was fully stretched, but over the middle of the river where the cables were closer together as the waters seemed at their wildest, hands and feet nearly touched and posteriors protruded! It was possible if you remembered the advice, "Don't look down!", but I assure you I prayed harder then ever.

'These same rivers can be negotiated and indeed could be put to positive use by the right kind of craft. Time and time again as I trekked along river banks or saw rivers from the road I was struck by their potential if the right kind of boat could be found. Many days were spent by doctors and nurses going out on foot to outlying clinics and dispensaries. That time could be used more profitably with patients — healing, treating, advising and giving help — if only their transport problems could be eased.'

Dr Graham Morris, director of the pioneering medical staff at Tansen Hospital, had also made me aware of the problems they faced. I wondered where they began with all the worms, scabies and sores, amongst the fevers, runs, fractures, bone infections and burns. There would be many cases of mothers with obstructed labour, others torn in delivery. The major problems were malnutrition, intestinal worms, gastro-enteritis, tuberculosis, leprosy and the children's diseases of measles, diphtheria and whooping cough. Staff members themselves were all well immunized and also sought to immunize the Nepalis if they could be reached.

Graham had shared with me the vision that he and

his medics had for the Palpa district.

'Four out of ten children in Nepal die before reaching the age of six due to disease and malnutrition. To help these children, we must go out and tackle first the physical barriers and then the barriers of suspicion. For us to convince them that our ways are better takes a lot of effort, patience and time. Some people think that Nepal doesn't have a lot of time before some major disaster hits her, in terms of famine and population explosion.

'Tansen, a long-established trading centre, is strategically situated in the centre of a large area, served by just one tortuous, twisting road, plus numerous tracks leading into the hills behind the town. Most of the patients arrive at the hospital either on someone's back or on a makeshift stretcher, often having journeyed for several days. Poor health is one of Nepal's main problems, compounded by inadequate communications. It is often impossible to communicate even between one valley and another. Road-building is a priority, but roads take many years to build and are often washed away in just a few moments in the monsoon season.

'I regard River Rover as a very interesting experiment. Up until now the rivers of Nepal have been considered obstacles to be overcome, not highways to be used. Such a craft may well prove relevant to this country's needs.'

Dick Matern had come to the Shanta Bhawan Mission Hospital in Kathmandu after working as a surgeon in war-torn Vietnam. He had a particular interest in children's congenital problems: club feet, cleft lip and palate, hernias, along with burns, scalds and fractures — 'all the junk that nobody bothers with much'. After visiting the expedition, Dick had told me, 'It distresses me that I spend so much of my time amputating the gangrenous and unset limbs of youngsters who have made their way eventually to

Kathmandu, seeking help. If just a little basic surgery was known in the villages, much needless suffering could be prevented. I would like to know where your hovercraft can take us medically.'

It seemed that Bill Gould's initial challenge to me was consistently being reinforced by other workers well-acquainted with conditions 'in the field'.

But was I being obstinate to pursue the medical aims of the expedition? On arrival at Kathmandu in early December, the Defence Attaché at the British Embassy, a Gurkha engineer officer, had counselled me to enjoy a challenging adventure but to remove all reference to medical matters and to forget the project's humanitarian and Christian aims. Team members who had travelled via Hong Kong, the location of the Brigade Headquarters of the British Gurkhas, had been left in no doubt that the sanity of our expedition was in question.

A struggle to survive is the everyday lot of the hill tribes from whom the Gurkha soldiers are recruited. The toughness, agility and courage of these sturdy warriors is the product of many generations of ekeing out a frugal living, perched high in the remote hills. The call to these hill tribesmen to be Gurkha soldiers has an innate and irresistible strength.

Into this Gurkha Army-dominated sphere comes an expedition led by an RAF officer, linked with a mission hospital health scheme, bringing a machine of innovative technology — an expedition also attempting to dispense medicine to the weak and helpless. A clash of purpose with the established order was inevitable. Lieutenant Colonel John Cross, District Recruiting Officer for the western region of Nepal, was already sending his Gurkha recruiters to the remote far west to seek out the genuine hill boy to maintain the line of fearless fighters. (I should add that Colonel Cross helped the expedition in many practical ways, even lending me his *sirdar*, head porter, to help organize an end-of-project trek to the headwaters of the Kali Gandaki.)

For the time being at least, our serious attempt to see if the hazards of the river could be overcome, opening up part of Nepal to swift medical help, would continue.

In the half-light of dawn, a gathering of Nepali folk waited for one of our track-suited doctors to open surgery. Children had burnt themselves in the fire during the night; dysentery was always rife. The short dentistry course which our doctors had taken as a precaution against team toothache was frequently put to good use on Nepalis of all ages. A blind Nepali walked for many days to our base seeking the restoration of his sight. After giving him a compo ration meal which he ate ravenously, we were able to refer him to Dr Graham Morris and the dedicated staff of the mission hospital at Tansen. A leprosy patient required an extensive and (for Nepal) expensive operation (£25) to enable him to walk again. The members of the expedition provided the cash for the cost price medicines needed and Graham's skilled hands restored his leg movements by a tendon-grafting operation.

Such faith in a team of British Servicemen was very humbling. Alas, sometimes the Nepalis looked for miracles from our doctors — miracles which could not be performed with the limited equipment available. 'The doctor understood the call but had not always wherewithal.'

Donald Bruce, our doctor from the Royal Navy, found the clinic at Base Camp an unforgettable experience:

'The news of our early morning clinic soon spread and thereafter we were awakened daily by a dawn chorus of Nepalis hacking and spitting *con spirito*. A visit to the doctor *sahibs* tended to be a family affair with cousins, sisters and aunts in attendance.

'We were confronted by a wide range of diseases, predominantly coughs, headaches and stomach pains, but also including some terrible burns and infections. Skin problems were particularly common — not surprising in a community where personal hygiene is not a priority. We saw more cases of scabies than we could treat, frequent infected skin lesions and babies covered with filthy, weeping impetigo. The worst cases were the burned or scalded children brought to us four or five days after the accident.

'Village Nepalis seem to believe that Western medicine provides an instant cure. They have difficulty in understanding the need for repeated dressings or a course of medicine lasting several days. We could undoubtedly have achieved more at Base Camp had patients heeded our appeals to return for treatment.

'We saw several severe abscesses, one of which was particularly noteworthy. An infant of two years, small for his age and unable to walk, was brought to the clinic. On questioning other mothers, it appeared that local children normally walked at between twelve and eighteen months. Examination of the child revealed a fluctuant mass with two crusted skin lesions on the right buttock. Liberally swabbing the area with dilute hibitane, I removed the crusts. After expressing as much pus as possible, the cavity was packed with hibitane wick, and the mother instructed to bring the child back for daily review. This advice was received with concern, for not only would it involve discomfort for the child, it would also mean her carrying the patient for a daily round trip of two hours on foot. She persevered for three days but then gave up. We never discovered the fate of that particular child. The infant mortality rate in Nepal is at least forty per cent, and it's not difficult to see why.

'Crippling ear and eye infections were readily

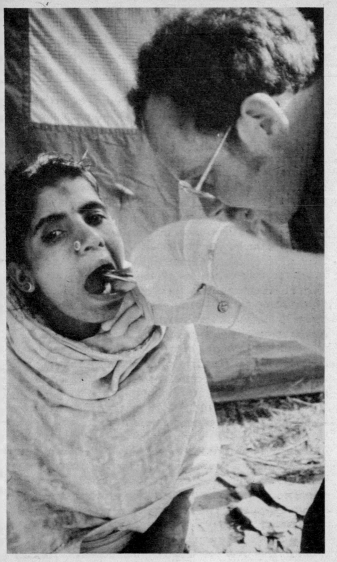

Much of Robin Dugdale's time in the clinics was
taken up with basic dentistry work.

cured by our antibiotics. A short course of the proper antibiotic also prevents deafness resulting from ear infection. My most impressive "cure" was a young man unable to see due to conjunctivitis who was back to normal within three days of starting the appropriate treatment.

'One aspect of health care, new to Robin and myself, was dentistry. With virtually no training, we readily began to extract teeth, although we were often unable to achieve good local anaesthesia. Many of our extractions must have been extremely painful but, on the whole, our patients seemed pleased with the results.

'Neither Robin nor I could speak Nepali, so we were dependent on our Gurkha Corporals Purna and Shovaram or the Sherpa staff for interpretation. All took this in good humour and with astonishing patience, for which Robin and I were very grateful. Trying to get Nepali womenfolk to take medicine for the first time was always a lengthy, coercive procedure. Working with the Nepalis was nearly always interesting and amusing, if occasionally irritating. Despite our work on their behalf, our patients rarely thanked us. Very occasionally, however, an egg (a valuable commodity) or a cauliflower would be presented to us, compensating for the more usual, outward at least, ingratitude. Nevertheless, practice back in the UK will seem tame after this.'

The relative proximity (four hours' trek) of our Base Camp to the mission hospital at Tansen meant that the experiences of this clinic were only a mild introduction to the untreated diseases, neglected wounds and unsplinted fractures which were to be encountered down-river. Interestingly, gratitude was more readily shown at the down-river clinics.

Purnasing failed to elicit the names for the cluster of huts on either side of the river at the first of those, at Camp 1. This camp, although only a day's walk from Ramdi, was in every way remote. Ours seemed to be the first white faces the people here had seen. The thatched huts with their red mud walls were ramshackle and in dire need of repair. The riverside fields looked parched and unyielding. The people wore drab, often frayed clothing, and the young boys' tattered shirts barely covered their midriffs; even the chickens looked scrawny. In spite of, or perhaps because of, their poverty, we were made particularly welcome. Their food was poor, their clothes were in rags and yet they chatted excitedly and could even manage a smile for those strange white men whose machine had sailed up out of the water on to their beach.

Dr Robin Dugdale found himself surrounded by a large crowd of Nepalis when he opened his clinic next morning:

'Many of the things I saw would have been trivial complaints at home, but neglect has meant that simple skin wounds have become life-threatening conditions. In most cases we applied simple dressings and attempted to combat the infections with antibiotics. I had reluctantly to turn away some without attempting treatment. An old soldier hobbled along with a leg fracture that had been left untreated and one leg was now four inches shorter than the other. I saw several cases of scabies: one small child's whole back and head were covered with sores. A few came to enjoy the show and to see what they could get out of us. Purnasing and I spent some time trying to unravel the story of one fit-looking young man. The smiles of those standing by eventually gave the game away.'

Whilst barely scratching the surface of a daunting task, that short stop may have saved a number of lives. As we saw the gratitude of the Nepalis for the limited help that Robin had been able to give them, we realized what a difference there could be if rudimentary medical help and instruction in hygiene were regularly available.

SEVEN

HOVERING DOCTORS

Our goal for January 1979, the period before the arrival of River Rover 02, was the thorough exploration of the fifty down-river miles which coincided with the border of the Palpa district. The nine miles below Ramdi were testing in both variety and difficulty of conditions, and were a fair sample of the white-water conditions River Rover could be expected to negotiate regularly. The pilots were becoming increasingly skilled at handling the craft and coping with the hazards of the Kali Gandaki.

We had established Camp 1 on a large sandbank just over nine miles downstream from base. From Ramdi, the site was a full day's trek of over twenty miles on narrow tracks. River Rover took just thirty-nine minutes to reach it. Across the river from the site was a high cliff, from which the villagers of the north bank often shouted to their neighbours on the south bank. Although the two villages were separated by only a few hundred yards, the communities were almost totally isolated from each other. The river causes this separation along most of its length. Except at the few bridging and ferrying points, the only people who

cross the river are the young men who take their lives
in their hands and swim across.

Another sixteen miles down-river, seventy
minutes by hovercraft, the site we chose for Camp 2
was less isolated. A ferryman plied his trade here, and
there was a small hamlet called Khoriya Ghat close to
the river. At the river's edge was a narrow mud
platform about one foot above river level, where we
parked the craft. Behind this an eight-foot bank
formed the edge of a large flat rock-bed, where we
would eventually pitch our tents. The five or six
houses of the village were further back from the river.
One of the buildings was temporarily empty and its
cool, dark interior, protected by the heavy shutter
planks used by the Nepalis instead of doors, was ideal
as a store. A local villager, Barboram, agreed to sleep
there and guard our supplies for a small daily consideration. Barboram was a likeable and honest character,
entering with gusto into the negotiations about his
wage-rate and conditions of service.

Gerry and Peter had the job of building up supplies
of fuel and food at Camp 2.

'Carrying a load of full four-and-a-half-gallon jerrycans was no problem,' Peter recalled later. 'A forty-
five-gallon drum, however, had to be emptied by
siphon tube into jerrycans and refilled on arrival at
Camp 2. We also used a siphon tube for transferring
fuel between outboard and integral fuel tanks on the
craft, and for mixing a proportion of aviation gasoline
into the local "cooking" fuel to improve its octane
rating for the hovercraft. Learning how to siphon fuel
is a speedy process — a mouthful of petrol concentrates
the mind wonderfully.'

We were not able to obtain regular radio communications with Camp 2. Our radio links — for logistic,
operational and safety purposes — were in the capable
hands of Royal Signals Officers Neil Fisher and John
Rollins. The link with the British Gurkha Centre at

Dharan, 250 miles away, enabled our messages to reach the UK the same day. However, the vital hovercraft net linking River Rover with base and the down-river camps was a most demanding requirement: the signal had to leapfrog from base at 2,000 feet over 7,000-foot obstacles back down to river level, on a range varying from one to seventy-five miles! The idiosyncrasies of this net often enabled clear contact with River Rover at fifty miles while failing to raise the craft round the first bend below Ramdighat.

Hovering easily onto the green river, we head back to base from Camp 2. Climbing over hump, Rover 01 is released from the power of the water's pull. In spite of the sunshine, the spray from these snow-fed waters is bitterly cold. Throttling back, Gerry gives the craft fine directive control at speed using the conventional rudder bars operated by his feet. A bend rapid quickly appears — it is a small one and we take it at speed on the shallow inside of the curve. The next rapid has been made more difficult by the construction of a fish-trap across the most convenient route. We head straight up the hill against the full flow of broken water. Ahead there is a rock in the middle dividing the river into two channels. We select our route and steer well clear.

We climb eight more rapids and pass the site chosen for Camp 1. The river is narrowing ahead and we slow down to select a safe path through. Back on the now-familiar but most difficult stretch we surge forward with confidence, gliding over the whirlpools which are so treacherous to boats. Rover 01 pitches in the roll of oncoming waves. The screen wipers are working hard to clear the swirl of water which gushes over the cabin. We head on through the thick of these challenging rapids, increasing power and using the elevons to steer a careful course. Pulling the stick fully back to maintain hover height and reducing speed at the same time, we carve our path through a testing boulder-strewn section. We reach nearly thirty-four knots on the long and enjoyable deep gorge section, against a water flow speed of fifteen knots. Guarding our approach to base is the most difficult rapid between Camp 2 and Ramdighat.

About a mile from base we turn the corner by the towering rock cliff. The water ahead boils and foams. As the gradient increases, Gerry applies full power to reach the maximum engine-speed of nearly 4,900 r.p.m. — equivalent to 70 m.p.h. on a motorway. A thumping noise we were to learn to dread came from the rear of the craft. Gerry cuts the revolutions to 3,600 and the noise fades. We slowly creep forward on reduced power and reach base.

'The Noise' was the only strictly mechanical difficulty with the hovercraft so far and had been causing us not a little concern. Returning from the day's first river crossing and applying full power to surge up the sandbank, we had had our first indication of a problem that was to test the resources and inventiveness of our engineers to the full. At high power settings when the ducted fans were heavily loaded, an irregular noise came from the rear of the craft. Initially it would only last for two or three seconds, but hour by hour it was to become more frequent and more severe until eventually the problem placed a limitation on the power available to the pilot. In the rapids we were tackling we needed every ounce of power.

We found that 'the Noise' seemed to coincide with a flapping vibration of the long-toothed propulsion belts as they passed over the aluminium pulleys. It seemed that we had a transmission problem. Lively discussion took place as to its cause and possible remedy. Engineer Doug Cooledge's initial reaction was that the problem was of our own making, since every other aspect of the craft was more than fulfilling its promise. For my part and applying my training as a geographer, I looked to the variables we had encountered in the terrain. What effect did the sharp sand have when fed through the transmission every time the craft came ashore? Or was the mica held in heavy solution in the waters of the Kali Gandaki causing the problem?

Noticeable wear had appeared on the aluminium pulleys so, advised by our engineers, I signalled Brian Holdsworth back in the UK to send replacements made of steel. I also recommended to Tim Longley that these stronger pulleys be incorporated in the now nearly complete Rover 02. Steel replacement pulleys were supplied to Gosport by Davall Gears of Hatfield within twenty-four hours of my signal reaching rear-party link leader Brian Holdsworth. Davall's managing director, Ken Johnston, had shown a keen interest in the project and I was now able to take up his generous offer to supply steel items for River Rover. The pulleys for 01 came out in the large pockets of Rick Elliott's duffle-coat, ranking as civil air cabin luggage, when four members of the advance part of the rear guard arrived at base on 19 January. This is one British firm which gives excellent attention to export orders, or perhaps 'export gifts' would be more accurate.

In the first three weeks of 1979, we modified and adjusted the transmission three times, and three times the symptoms reappeared. We eagerly awaited the arrival of those steel replacement pulleys. The role of our engineers in the expedition was becoming much more important than I could have envisaged. Doug Cooledge and Bruce Vincent worked long hours into the night to keep River Rover operational during the day, painstakingly searching out possible remedies to the belt slip. They became experts at dismantling the transmission system 'in the field' and adept at adjusting the belts to a fine tolerance.

Throughout this period we continued our exploration downstream, making regular visits to Camp 2. We were exhilarated at the success of the craft in just the conditions for which it had been designed. We

When designer Tim Longley flew out to join the expedition in Nepal, he saw at last the fruit of his hard work.

were driving along stretches of river that had never been travelled by any means of transport. We were able to average speeds of 25 m.p.h., and succeeded, on one run, in reaching Khoriya Ghat in just over one hour, returning against the flow of the river in one hour twenty minutes. A two days' journey on foot had been reduced to one of just over an hour by hovercraft. As an encouragement, I signalled this exciting progress to Tim, now busy putting the finishing touches to Rover 02, back at Gosport, including the incorporation of the steel transmission pulleys.

We intended to check out our claim that half an hour by River Rover equalled a full day's trek. On Monday 8 January, we fused old and new styles of exploration: a small trekking party set out across the narrow tracks to rendezvous with Gerry and the hovercraft crew down-river at Camp 1. As the trekkers gulped hot cups of tea, finished a hasty breakfast and secured rucksacks, the first of the Nepali patients for the morning clinic appeared noiselessly among us.

Travel in Nepal is almost entirely on foot, and it's not uncommon for porters to carry loads of 160 pounds. In contrast to the Nepalis who carry their loads suspended from their foreheads by strong rope-bands, we carried our light twenty-five-pound pack of essentials in rucksacks. The two Sherpas who accompanied us on this trek also seemed to prefer rucksacks. 'It's a matter of status,' I was told. Porters carry rope-bands and baskets — experienced Sherpas now carry rucksacks!

We climbed out through the silvery mist into the bright morning sunshine, along a winding track through small rice terraces. We paused to allow a file of bullocks to pass down to Ramdi, encouraged by a small barefoot boy brandishing a stick of sugar-cane. Having delivered the bullocks, he would certainly devour the stick. After a stiff climb to the rim of the valley, we were rewarded with an unhindered, cloud-free view of the spectacular snow-clad giants of the western Himalayas. The steeple peak of Machhapuchhare at 23,000 feet, though not the highest, is certainly the most prominent.

We now turned east to clamber back down the trail to the riverside. On reaching the water, our undulating route followed the river for about three miles. Although we were travelling *down* the river gradient, we discovered that the ups seem to outnumber the downs! Just after 10.30 a.m., we rested on a large rock outcrop jutting into the river to enable our Sherpas to have their *daalbaat*. Hearing the unmistakable hum of River Rover we turned to see Rover 01 appear as a glinting dot at the head of the long straight gorge. After plunging through the rapid at the entrance to the gorge, it glided gently over a section of fast shallows before turning in a graceful sweep to settle on a sand spit below our rocky seat.

In the warm sunshine and the sparkling morning light, we all felt elated. As Gerry clambered up to our rock perch, there was a note of pride in his voice: 'We've made good time Mike — we left Ramdi just fifteen minutes ago!' Extracting a primus stove from Rover's freight hold, Paddy brewed us a strong pot of tea. Shirts came off and we lazed a little. Paddy threw a pebble or two at a submerged rock. They didn't bounce. The 'rock' was the bloated body of a young girl. We tossed the remainder of our tea away, the euphoria of our morning shattered.

As River Rover disappeared down-river round the long sweep towards the next rapid, we made the faintest radio contact with base, then the trekkers moved off. We resumed our journey in thoughtful mood, somewhat confused by the numerous animal trails which criss-crossed our intended track. We headed off to climb another ridge, the roar of the nearby river keeping us in the right general direction.

Our pathway zig-zagged, linking the small hamlets dotted precariously along the ridge high above the river, and we paused to exchange greetings with the peasants who somehow manage to eke out a living on these steepest of slopes. Late in the afternoon we reached the slope above Camp 1. River Rover, the orange tents and the smoke of the camp fire were visible far below. A rough-hewn stairway led down to the river. We dropped from the shimmering sunshine into the cool shadows.

Seven and a half hours after leaving base at Ramdi, we were more than grateful to reach Camp 1 and down a liberal quantity of hot, sweet tea. In the time we had taken to complete the trek, Gerry and Peter had made two round River Rover trips to base, erected the tents, and helped Robin to sort out his medical stores as well as preparing the evening meal!

Other team members also had the opportunity of experiencing the rigours of trekking in Nepal. Neil Fisher, one of the stalwarts of the advance party, was required back at his Gurkha Signals Squadron in Brunei before the end of January. I wanted him to leave on a high note and so asked him to lead the first of three planned treks, taking a small exploration team to report on the northern reaches of the Kali Gandaki between Beluwa and Jomosom in the Mustang. It might be worthwhile in future years to carry the pre-fabricated parts of a hovercraft to these remote locations for assembly on site and I needed some first-hand assessment of this possibility.

Neil takes up the story:

'The trip itself was against the clock. This time restriction and the distances involved meant that choice of companions was important for such a physic-ally demanding exercise. I was joined by Stuart Forbes, Gurkha Corporal Shovaram and Sherpa Kembahadur. I made sure that the two Nepali had enough *baat*

(Nepali curry) in compo to last them for two weeks, and Stuart and I took enough British compo for eight days, along with enough money to buy a meal in some of the larger bazaars we would go through.

'We left Base Camp in the minibus at 07.00 hours on 30 December 1978, alighting at the Gurkhas' Welfare Centre to the north of Syangja. From there we planned to head west, via a village called Darung to meet the River Kali Gandaki at Beluwa. (At Darung I was hoping to find Signalman Govinde Gurung, on leave from my troop in Brunei.)

'The average rucksack weighed seventy pounds when we started out. Just to get to the river, we had to climb up over 3,000 feet then 3,000 feet down the other side. It would be difficult to get to know the rest of the team in these circumstances — as the slog got harder and steeper, so each individual became lost in his own thoughts. Every half-hour we stopped at a *chautare* for a rest. These are three-tiered rectangular collections of stones where the tired traveller could sit down on one tier and rest his load on the next, thus easing his shoulders without having to remove his pack.

'When we reached Darung, Govinde was waiting for me, having been forewarned by a little boy I had met and chatted to on the trail. No matter what panic this message may have brought — that his old *sahib* was not 7,000 miles away in the steamy jungle of Brunei but coming up the hill to see him — he showed none, and was the perfect host. We were given *baat* by Govinde's mother and entertained by the local band. As we left the next morning, Govinde garlanded us and presented me with a *kukri* (the special Gurkha knife). I was quite overwhelmed by the hospitality and genersoity we had received.

'At 6,000 feet, at the lip of the Darung valley, we looked north up the Gandaki valley. Although the Himalayas were fifty miles away, we still had to raise our eyes to see their majestic peaks. We got up early on

New Year's Day to watch the fantastic sight of the sun hitting Dhaulagiri and Annapurna. We had to walk between these two — that was where the river cascaded down from 10,000 feet to just 6,000 feet in little less than fifteen miles.

'By nightfall we were not far from Baglung and we camped by the river, all feeling quite tired as the pace was beginning to tell. We did not reach Tatapani until a day later than I had planned, causing Shov great agitation as we had to camp near the trail. His was a real fear because the trails were used a great deal by Tibetan tinkers, peddlars and "merchants". They carried a whole arsenal of knives and were a fearsome sight, dressed in their Tibetan boots and black robes, topped by long, straggly black hair and moustaches.

'By Tatapani the river had just descended 4,000 feet in about ten miles and we had to climb that on 4 January, our hardest day yet. The steep climb didn't level off until Ghae; when we reached there, we had effectively walked "through" the Himalayas. At Lete we crossed the river on one of the numerous rickety wire bridges. Round the next spur, we discovered that we had surmounted the steepest part of the gorge and were now on the more gently sloping plateau of the Mustang.

'Because of the height of the Mustang, the closeness of the Indian plain and the large temperature differential between the two, convection causes great quantities of air to move up and down the gorge. In the mornings, the cold air of the Mustang sweeps down the gorge, and in the afternoons, the hot air of the plain rushes up it. Far from being pleasant breezes, these are full-blooded gales — natural phenomena of the Himalayas. We were caught in a dust-storm whipped up by one such gale as we set off for Jomosom, a bleak lonely spot at a height of nearly 10,000 feet. Six miles north of Jomosom is Keg Beni, the start of the thirty-miles area forbidden to foreigners.

'We started on the return journey on Saturday 6 January and trekked via Kalopari, a small village near Lete, to Tatapani, Pokhara and back to base. Our food had just lasted; we had coped with the dreaded "runs" — an inevitable problem for all the team throughout the expedition; we were fitter, stronger, lighter and now working well as a team, despite feeling the worse for wear. In thirteen days we had walked 146 miles, climbed 23,000 feet, descended 21,000 feet and completed the mission Mike had given us.

'Our river reconnaissance report was divided into three widely differing sections:

'**Beluwa to Beni** The water level in these twenty miles was dropping rapidly during the early days of January, uncovering many hazardous boulders. River Rover would be able to navigate both ways on this section from October until the arrival of the monsoon the following June. The torrent of fast-flowing, monsoon-fed water would not be a barrier to the hovercraft riding free on its cushion of air, but the floating debris (trees, flotsam, bullocks, even houses) would make navigation dangerous and unwise.

'**Beni to Lete** The river falls nearly 5,000 feet in eighteen miles between Lete and Beni and a foaming cauldron of white water cascades down a track of ever-increasing severity. Only dead men would ever ride those cataracts.

'**Lete to Jomosom** Being in the Himalayan rain-shadow, this area is protected from the ravages of the monsoon. The river up here on the Mustang would be easily navigable throughout the year by hovercraft, although perhaps a little low on water. The floor of the giant gorge is relatively flat and wide, the river gradient gradual. In 1972, Michel Peissel had successfully taken his single-seat sport hovercraft on part of this stretch.

'Beyond Jomosom must remain speculation.'

Neil's essential setting-up tasks were completed; he
had trekked through the Himalayas and seen where
his soldiers came from, how they lived and what
motivated them. He now had to return to his officer's
responsibilities in Brunei. We also had to bid farewell
to Base Camp Commander Dennis Cooper, who left for
the UK on 7 January. His diplomatic and language skills
had been invaluable in securing our relatively painless
entry into Nepal and in promoting excellent public
relations with village leaders, thus ensuring a court-
eous welcome for us to the banks of the sacred Kali
Gandaki.

Our colleagues left reluctantly and we were sorry to
see them go. It seemed, however, that our Base Camp
was the scene of arrivals as well as departures. Local
village elders, wearing the official black, stiff Nepali
cap, were frequent and welcome guests. Although
these high caste Brahmins are forbidden to eat at our
'unclean' table, they easily succumbed to the lure of
Army hard tack biscuits, liberally smeared with
strawberry jam and washed down with hot, sweet tea.

Groups of Nepali women in their embroidered
shawls and skirts would often gather round our
strange craft. We became used to seeing the dazzling
array of gold jewellery which adorned these women.
Nepali men distrust the idea of handing over their
wealth to the custody of a bank for safe keeping — the
wife is her husband's walking bank account. Even a
poorly-clad woman would be wearing precious
armlets, ear-rings, necklaces and prominent nose
studs.

We were also able to give those interested in the
feasibility of using hovercraft in Nepal the opportunity to ride the rapids and check for themselves! Carl
Johansson, the executive secretary of the Nepal United
Mission, experienced the white water for himself. I
also issued invitations to all the relevant senior British
Gurkha officers. Captain John Rogers of the 1/2nd King

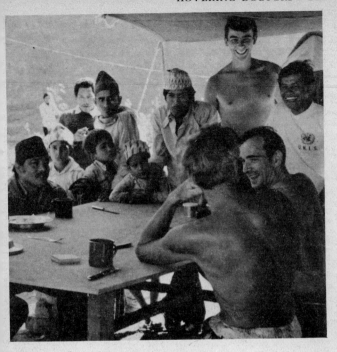

High caste Brahmins should have stayed separate
from our camp, but tasty jam and biscuits encourage
them to visit us!

Edward the Seventh's Own Gurkha Rifles was the first Gurkha officer stationed in Nepal to travel in River Rover. He was impressed by his trip early in January on the 'hairier' section of the river. Senior officials in Kathmandu were less willing actually to undertake firsthand experience.

Both the medical staff from the Tansen Hospital and the engineers of the Mission Technical Institute at Butwal were welcome visitors to Ramdi. We were pleased to share our camp meal and then our hovercraft in action with these selfless people. It gave us the opportunity to return hospitality but of more importance, it enabled these front-line workers to share the potential of River Rover for the country of their adoption. Together they represented Australia, New Zealand, Canada, Norway, Sweden, USA and the United Kingdom. There were many more women than men.

While the church in the West debates the role of women in leadership in the home situation, women have quietly and without fuss been working on the mission front line in a ratio of seven women to three men. We knew a little of what these dedicated girls have to cope with. A lone nurse will set up a simple dispensary in the heart of a remote village, surrounded by sick and needy people. A few feet away, a skinny cow splashes droppings on to her rucksack containing the life-saving medicines. A mother is combing lice from her daughter's hair and the debris is falling close to a cooking-pot. A dung cake has been applied to a deep wound. A brave girl from the West is prepared to tackle situations which would make a strong man wince. Having saved many lives she will return to Tansen exhausted, possibly suffering from amoebic dysentry, hepatitis or one or another of the 'nasties' which all who stay in Nepal any length of time inevitably succumb to. After a short recuperation, she'll be back to the life-saving task of love.

Lieutenant John Rollins was an expert canoeist as well as a skilled radio operator. The waters of the Kali Gandaki have all the plunging twists and undertows which can easily take the life of all but the most expert in a canoe. John was ever ready to pit his skills against this river. With our mission visitors and numerous astonished Nepalis lining the river, John gave a river spectacular, capsizing and rolling his canoe in the centre of the formidable Base Camp rapid. We became alarmed at the seeming length of time John remained inverted until he eventually rolled upright, with the minimum of fuss. Our visitors never tired of this grandstand afternoon: John's canoe exploits, hovercraft experience for the adults and rides in Gemini for the mission children as only Tony Maher can give them.

Smiling mission engineer Sam Rouhoniemi, an American Methodist, visited Base Camp and pressed for a trip in River Rover over the most testing rapids. Unknown to us, Sam was suffering from terminal cerebral cancer. After the trip, he talked enthusiastically about the potential of the craft and gave our engineers some helpful advice on the production of spare hovercraft parts from local materials. Sam stuck to his God-appointed task to the very end. He died in Nepal, two days before our expedition concluded.

Around this time we were expecting a visitor of a rather different kind — although the purpose of her visit was also to see and assess River Rover. BBC assistant producer Jenny Cropper arrived on the last flight of the day to Pokhara on 11 January. Working with *The World About Us* team has made Jenny a veteran of travel to remote places; at Pokhara, the grazing cattle had to be cleared from the grass airfield before her plane could land! The provision of exclusive toilet and washing facilities at Base Camp were the only concessions we could allow for Jenny, the only woman on the team. She expected no more; she faced the filth, disease and ravages as well as the infinite beauty of the sub-drenched sights of this river as an equal.

Jenny was keen to signal her first impressions of River Rover and the Kali Gandaki to producer Tony Salmon, stranded in London by a strike of BBC camera crews. Next day we paused in our down-river explorations to take Jenny on the spectacular up-river gauntlet to the White House. The water level had fallen alarmingly during the short period since our last operations here and this test track was becoming progressively more difficult. Despite her conditioning through previous exposure to high drama, Jenny found the adrenalin flowing strongly as she sat in the front passenger seat of Rover 01!

We now planned to undertake our longest down-river excursion yet, aiming to explore the full length of the Kali Gandaki along the northern flank of the Mahabharat as far as Khālte, where the river takes its irrevocable plunge south. River Rover had already been as far as Umse, forty-five miles down-river from Ramdi, completing the ninety-mile round trip in just under eight hours and impressing us with its economical fuel consumption of two and a half gallons per hour. The journey to Khālte would be sixty unhurried miles each way; Jenny Cropper planned to use the trip to observe suitable vantage-points for the BBC cameras to record our proposed journey next month — the full seventy-five miles to Narayanghat in the Terai.

Food, clean water, tentage, tools, spare fuel, freshly-charged batteries for the radio, compass, space blanket and first aid kit are all stored on board to cater for possible emergency. The river route on our map will be checked. An overnight camp down-river is planned.

Below Umse the river becomes wider, but only marginally less forceful as it evolves into large, green-blue sweeps bounded by sheer rock cliffs on one side and wide, uncovered boulder-fields on the other. The rapids are confined to the bends and are negotiated by River Rover without difficulty At Khālte, where the river turns sharply south, the Mahabharat Heights have closed in and the angry roar of quickening water echoes in the enclosed valley ahead. Gerry engages with the swirls and waves as he hovers into the depths of this gorge. It is mid-afternoon and Rover is sixty-three miles from base. Time to head back up-river. After three miles, Gerry finds a convenient shelf near Khālte — a likely site for a future Camp 3 — and an ideal stop for the night. Radio contact with base is loud and clear.

A friendly, slightly nervous crowd of Nepalis immediately surrounds the crew. Some have never seen a white face before, let alone a hovercraft. Sweets are given to the children. The people quickly warm to the strangers and are most helpful. After the evening meal cooked on an open fire using damp driftwood, a number of our empty food tins are handed to the villagers squatting nearby. In the morning a man with a smooth, round face appears with one of the tins filled with freshly boiled milk. He refuses payment for this unsolicited act of friendship. The gift of buffalo milk makes a satisfying addition to the routine breakfast of beans, burgers and oatmeal blocks.

We regularly encountered this spontaneous kindness. On one occasion, Gerry was trying to reach base before the onset of darkness when a piece of debris went through River Rover's lift fan. His crew couldn't continue on, and faced an uncomfortable night with only emergency space blankets for protection. But the riverside people arrived, built a large fire and provided rush mats and rough wool blankets. They even brought rum to drink and would probably have looked after the team for several days!

Early morning radio contact with base is just about audible. By 10 a.m., Rover is passing Camp 2, but Gerry keeps the revolutions below 4,000 as when the throttle is fully opened there is the faintest sign of belt slip. After nursing the transmission for a further ten miles, he beaches the craft and sets about adjusting the belt tension, before returning triumphantly, if a little tired, to base. A return journey of 126 miles has been accomplished.

Driver training was meanwhile continuing for all the team in our small inflatable Skima 4 hovercraft, using the fast-flowing stretches of water above and below Ramdi. Doug Couledge and Bruce Vincent were becoming confident Skima drivers, to the extent of giving others the odd piece of handling advice. Together they took Skima 4 under the shadow cast by the girders of Ramdi bridge and into the section above the Vicarage Lawn where the narrow river was encased by vertical rock walls. At the head of this ravine was a tantalizing rapid with water flowing in opposing directions — an obstacle which River Rover always treated with caution.

Attempting to take Skima 4 through this barrier, they managed to stall all three two-stroke engines. Despite furious pulling on the starting toggles, the engines failed to respond. Fortunately the inflatable hull of Skima 4 was well-built to take the punishment that followed. The craft was swept down-river out of control, bouncing off the rock walls like a ball on a bagatelle table, to be deposited conveniently on the sandbank of the Vicarage Lawn. Having tried to push back new frontiers, they now had several hours of skirt and engine repairs!

Gerry was also busy giving Peter Dixon concentrated tutoring on the most unyielding sections of the river, passing on his finely-tuned skills at Rover's controls in readiness for the second craft's arrival.

Our thoughts turned to home, our families and the two sections of the rear party as we met for prayer and a short reading on Sunday 14 January. For many in

the team, the motivating force behind the whole
project was their Christian faith and their love for Jesus
Christ. We committed to God's care the four who
would be leaving the UK that day at breakfast-time.

EiGHT

THE FINAL FRONTIERS

On 19 January 1979, in the middle of a downpour, we welcomed the first half of the rear link party to base. Sergeant Rick Elliott and Corporal Mick Reynolds, both of REME, were accompanied by BP-sponsored Hugh Bennell, and Plessey engineer Ed Chase. In the deep pockets of Rick Elliott's duffle-coat were the precious steel pulleys.

Rick and Mick were opposites in temperament, attitude and outlook: Rick was inventive, outgoing and extrovert; Mick was thoughtful, attentive and diligent. Strong characters in their different ways, both had a wholehearted commitment to the goal of the project. The strange sad sights of this Mahabharat river were to get beneath the skin of both these tough, versatile, soldier engineers. I had to gently dissuade Rick from seeking to adopt an orphan boy who frequented Base Camp. On returning to the UK, Mick wrote to me: 'My experience amongst the Nepalis has helped me to put the trivial upsets of life in perspective.'

Hugh Bennell, at nineteen, was six years below the minimum age recommended for members of an arduous expedition such as ours. Hugh had been partially supported by the BP 'Young Explorers' Scheme'. He had raised the balance of his contribution by working long hours navvying on motorway construction. Someone prepared to work like that to reach a goal seemed to me to have just the spirit of application appropriate for the tests of this river. The inclusion of Hugh was a calculated risk — but one which was to bring a dividend to both the expedition and the Royal Air Force. Without any coercion, Hugh joined the RAF at the end of the project and is now undergoing training as a fast jet pilot.

Plessey engineer and Cambridge graduate Ed Chase had given much of his spare time to the project since the building of the Missionnaire for Lake Chad in 1970. Ed has strong practical engineering skills, but his academic-based appreciation of the field tasks did not always marry in with the down-to-earth approach of other team members. For Ed, the time in Nepal was to be a testing period of special preparation, an apprenticeship which he bore stoically. Only God knew at that time that Ed would be selected, along with TEAR Fund worker Bernard Coleman, for the essential task of taking the project through to its fulfilment in Irian Jaya later in the year.

In many reports of major expeditions, I had read of the aggravation between the journalists and cameramen and the leadership of the expedition. So it was with mixed feelings that I anticipated the arrival of the BBC's *World About Us* team. They would be seeking to make a high-quality, exciting and telling film of our exploits. I needed to keep the expedition heading for its goal but was also keen for our contest with the river to be well recorded, particularly for those we couldn't persuade to visit our location in the middle hills.

On 30 January, producer Tony Salmon, cameramen Ian Stone and John Beck and sound recordist Mervyn

Broadway joined Jenny Cropper at Base Camp. Accompanying them was a Nepalese Liaison Officer.

The recently-resolved industrial dispute at the BBC, which had complicated their travel arrangements, had spotlighted the expense of keeping a camera crew in the field. It was as though Tony Salmon had a fast-ticking taxi meter in his rucksack. It speeded up to time-and-a-half or double-time for evening and early morning use of the camera team. This seemed incongruous in our timeless riverside situation, where distance and time is measured in days' trekking and the only clock is the rising and setting of the sun.

Any apprehensions I may have had about these representatives of the media were unfounded. They moulded so well into the expedition setting that I subconsciously considered them as part of the team. On their own initiative, Ian, John and Mervyn built a bamboo bridge from the bank of the river at base to a most convenient sandbank which the falling water level had uncovered. This provided an ideal hovercraft landing stage, and we all appreciated the BBC bridge. The co-operation which developed between the expedition and the BBC team was mutually felt, as an appreciative letter I subsequently received from Tony Salmon clearly indicated. This harmony remained throughout, despite our different emphases.

The television team spent two days capturing the sights and sounds of the local people searching for a living in the harsh riverside environment: men fishing with dams and basket traps or smashing stones on the rocks and stunning the sheltering fish; other Nepalis undertaking the perilous crossing of the river in dugout canoes; burdened porters filing past journeying as far afield as Tibet, carrying firewood, sacks of rice, live chickens, pottery, heavy timber or even people on their backs.

Tony — ever-mindful of his budget — wanted to film the major sequence down-river to Narayanghat

The two craft operated successfully together for five weeks.

first, using just one River Rover (01), and conclude with local cultural scenes and the spectacular up-river stretches from Ramdighat to the White House. I wanted to await the arrival of Rover 02 before mounting the thrust to break out of the Mahabharat range. The second craft was an essential part of my plans for the next stage.

In the event Rover 01 dictated the outcome. A breakdown en route to Camp 1 made it vital to replace the aluminium pulleys. There followed forty hours of total application by the engineers, led by Doug Cooledge and Bruce Vincent, on a precision problem to be performed with the minimum of workshop equipment. Doug refused to be hurried — a mistake could take Rover 01 off the water for a week or more. He sweated the aluminium pulleys off the steel shaft using a paraffin heater. That night, my mind concentrated on the hovercraft and the river, I slept fitfully and wandered into our workshop tent on several occasions. Kept awake by mugs of steaming tea and helped by a rota of assistants, Doug was slowly but certainly making progress. At 2.30 p.m. the next day, the job was finished.

Back in Gosport, the 'faithful remnant' — designer Tim Longley and engineers Bernard Coleman and Tony Burgess — were also beavering away, working long hours to ensure that Rover 02 was ready for lift-off from RAF Lyneham on 30 January by Ascot flight 5475. Work had started on the second craft on 6 October the previous year. We had been able to employ versatile craftsman Dennis Ling. With volunteer help from Trevor Cave and Dennis Adams and the off-duty contribution of several expedition team members, Rover 02 was completed on time for take-off. It had required 2,000 manufacturing hours at Gosport and was finished in fifteen working weeks.

Rear-link leader Commander Brian Holdsworth

signalled to me on 26 January that the flight for Kathmandu — albeit with minimal freight space — was on.

I had selected forty-nine-year-old Brian to lead the rear party delivering Rover 02 on the basis of his wide Service experience, his equanimity, stability and unhurried attention to detail. His rear-link duties included oversight of the seven-man group working fourteen-hour days at Gosport to complete 02's construction, air cargo documentation, fielding the flow of signals I sent from Ramdighat and liaising with RAF Air Movements on progress towards Flight 5475.

Hazardous driving conditions in the arctic UK winter of 1978-79, the Christmas and New Year holiday 'shutdown' and a rash of national strikes gave Brian a Herculean task. Besides these external forces, naval medics had found an irregularity in his heartbeat. A less resilient spirit would have had every justification for giving up the struggle. But Brian had caught a glimpse of the visionary nature of the project which saw him through the eventful days prior to departure:

'My immediate problem was the availability and timing of the Hercules flight. Prospects during the second week of December were distinctly unpromising! Expeditions — even Joint Service ones led by RAF Officers — are not high on the list of airlift priorities! But my good friend in Air Movements, Bill Underwood, came up with a date, 30 January, which I immediately accepted. I knew deep down we would not get a better offer.

'Following the departure of the "advance guard" on 14 January, I spent long hours checking, sorting, packing, weighing, measuring, labelling, listing, and driving long journeys to collect strike-bound equipment. The cargo list handed over to me in December by Mike Cole included a secondhand operating-table which the expedition was to give to Tansen Mission Hospital where the hovercraft project had been conceived. Mike was keen that we should include such things in our cargo, and the list was subsequently expanded after he had witnessed firsthand the desperate needs of the medical workers. In particular, our stand-by generator could provide life-saving electricity to an isolated dispensary at Okhadunga. There were many amendments to the cargo list but the real priority never changed: item 1 on the list was River Rover 02, 1,800 pounds.

'When I visited the RAF 38 Group Cargo Allocation Centre at Upavon on Thursday 25 January for a final check, I sensed that a crisis was developing. HMS *Hydra* on station in the Indian Ocean and heading for Bombay needed a replacement for one of her main engines, and the RAF unit in Hong Kong wanted a spare Hercules engine. The only transport aircraft available to satisfy this priority operational requirement was our Hercules. Everyone was very sorry but expeditions were a low priority for airlift, and only a minimal amount of our freight could go on Flight 5475. I did a lot of telephoning, emphasizing that the main objectives of the expedition would be difficult to achieve unless River Rover 02 got to Nepal. I received plenty of sympathy but little else at that stage. Good old Bill Underwood told me not to give up hope . . . both he and I have been around a long time! In faith I gave the go-ahead for all our freight to be assembled at Lyneham on Friday as planned, and supervised the movement myself. Then I went home for a weekend of prayer and to get myself ready for Nepal.

'On return to Lyneham on Monday, I learned that the mighty Hydra diesel engine had been rejected as unsafe cargo. Tremendous sigh of relief. The Hercules spare engine still had to go, but it seemed that all our freight could be fitted in. The duty air cargo team did a splendid job preparing the loading of our cargo. The pallet containing boxes with River Rover on top was a masterpiece. Together with Tim Longley, Tony Burgess and Bernard Coleman, the last of the Gosport workers, I settled into Flight 5475 at 03.00 on Tuesday 30 January.

'The journey out east was comparatively relaxing: our rear party was ready for a rest. I have always been a contented Hercules passenger — I like to be able to take a good long walk whilst airborne! Overnight stops were at Akrotiri and Bombay. On landing at Kathmandu on the evening of 1 February, feeling rather pleased with ourselves, we were greeted by Mike, several of his (by now) Nepali old hands — and an electricity power cut.'

Thirty-six hours after arrival at Kathmandu, Rover 02 was sitting proudly in pristine condition on the river bank of Ramdi. Negotiations through customs had been quick and easy: Rover 01 had paved the way — Rover 02 followed smoothly. A simple rule of Eastern customs routine is that if it has been done before, then the precedent has been set!

It was an emotional moment for me, as I spoke to the complete team in the field, BBC included, for the first time. With designer Tim Longley now with us, a lively debate ensued amongst the engineers as to the cause of the belt slip we had experienced.

At dawn on Sunday 4 February, ten of the team gathered round a chalice of fruit juice and a plate of broken hard tack biscuits in a simple act of communion to remember the death of Jesus Christ our Lord who had brought us thus far. All was still in the early morning hush except for the unquenchable roar of Base Camp rapid. The BBC noiselessly recorded our act of worship and dedication. Afterwards, at breakfast, Brian Holdsworth took up his duties in charge of base. Brian had many years of Navy service behind him, but even his experienced eyes were to be surprised by the strange sights of this Mahabharat river.

The long hours of the Gosport working routine continued for two more days, and for Rick Elliot one night as well, as we prepared to launch Rover 02. The engine for the second hovercraft was as yet unused. At dusk on the second day after its arrival, and with the craft securely tethered to rocks, the familiar hum could be heard from the bank — for the first time from Rover 02. With differing throttle settings, Rick spent the next twelve hours ensuring that the engine was river-ready. I was lulled to sleep to the tune of the 20TL and it was still going when Rambahadur Lama brought me my pre-dawn mug of steaming, hot, sweet tea.

For Tim Longley, who had worked so long and hard on the hovercraft design, the launch of 02 was a memorable occasion:

'My introduction to the Kali Gandaki river was on the maiden flight of 02, the second River Rover, which I had accompanied out to Nepal. Time had prevented us from testing this particular craft under more congenial conditions, and so I was unanimously elected to be the "observer" accompanying Gerry Bradnam, the chief pilot, when the craft was first launched into the turbulent tail-race of a rapid. For the next half-hour, the craft and I were introduced to the thrills of skimming upstream and downstream over rock-strewn rapids, while we also tried to concentrate on such mundane matters as engine performance and control response.

'Two hours later I was again aboard 02, this time in formation with Mike Cole and Peter Dixon in River Rover 01, on our way down-river to a village twelve miles away at Camp 1, where the expedition doctors had been assessing the medical needs of the people and doing what little they could to help. The journey took thirty-five minutes. The local people allow one and a half days to reach this village, trekking on foot over the mountain trails! We were greeted warmly by Tony Maher and Stuart Forbes, who were manning Camp 1 permanently at that time.

'The return journey upstream also took thirty-five

minutes, and was the more exhilarating because in the eyes of the Nepalis lining the river banks we were doing the impossible.'

This was a very significant moment for the relationship which I had developed with Tim Longley through the trials, setbacks and encouragements of the last four years. This friendship had been primary to the whole endeavour. Tim had now witnessed his craft performing the special rapid-climbing task which very many had thought and others had frankly said was not possible. Observing a trace of moisture in Tim's grateful eyes, I thought of the quotation that runs, 'Those who say it can't be done are sometimes interrupted by others doing it.'

With the arrival of Rover 02, the scope of our operation had more than doubled. However, it had set a poser for Gerry Bradnam. There were no traffic regulations for amphibious hovercraft on this river. If 01 approached 02 from the opposite direction, which side should they pass? It was decided that the rule of the sea (keep right) would apply on the river, and that should they pass on a beach, then we would adhere to the British rule of the road (keep left). Without such rules of operation the bizarre might just happen, with the only two craft operating in this wild isolated terrain actually colliding!

The following morning, Wednesday 7 February, the journey to Narayanghat began. This was a serious attempt to see if the only two roads in the area could be linked by our River Rover craft, thus providing the possibility of swift medical help in this isolated region. The thin blue line on our map failed to show the furies of the river as it sought to breach the Mahabharat.

On the BBC's behalf, I had arranged for a four-hour hire of a Royal Nepal Airlines Allouette helicopter to undertake aerial photography. The chopper was due at Base Camp on 9 February, and I would guide it down-river to Camp 2 by mid-morning. Hopefully Robin would have concluded his riverside clinic and the hovercraft journey on towards the Mahabharat ravine could go ahead, complete with a film record from the air. I was also eager to get an aerial view of the river track to the north towards Annapurna. The pilot discarded the doors of the Allouette to facilitate easy filming and headed north. Plucked out in my light clothing from the riverside, I was unprepared for the hover high above the river as it curved through the Himalayas. This spectacular experience was only mildly marred by the chatter of my teeth.

Critics of the hovercraft project have sometimes taken me to task concerning helicopters, proposing that they can do at least as much as the River Rover hovercraft in helping the sick. But a quick look at the running costs puts a different light on the matter: I bonded $375 US per hour to secure the Allouette. River Rover operates for $10 per hour, fuel included. Moreover, the basic cost of a basic helicopter is at least twelve times that of River Rover!

Peter Dixon was in the driver's seat of Rover 02 for the journey to Narayanghat:

'My role, pilot of the second hovercraft, was a stunning and exacting experience. With the camera crew on board, I kept as close to the other craft as I dared in a vehicle which has no brakes.

'Part of the purpose of our journey was to assess the medical problem in some of the remote locations down-river and the feasibility of holding clinics at the riverside, so Robin held a clinic at each of our camps. Inevitably the camps were crowded for as long as we were there, with the local villagers flocking to gaze at the foreigners and to be cured of their ills.

'I was collecting firewood near our second camp when I heard the sound of drums and horns and saw a procession on the high ridge above the river-bank. When I reached camp, the group had also arrived and

On his trips as the expedition surveyor, David Porter sketched the local Nepalis, capturing their character very clearly.

were waiting to cross the river by dug-out canoe. The procession was escorting a bride being taken to her groom; she was carried hidden in a brightly-coloured hammock suspended from a bamboo pole. The band played as they waited, with giant curved horns up to five feet high, and a diverse selection of home-made drums. Later that evening, their delivery completed, they returned to play by our camp fire.

'The morning and early afternoon of the next day were spent climbing rapids for the benefit of the cameraman in the Allouette helicopter. Both hover-craft left Camp 2 later in the day on the long stretch to Deoghat (Camp 4) near Narayanghat. The final testing fifteen miles of this run had not previously been attempted.

'We swept by Khālte, the selected site for Camp 3, and were expecting to reach Deoghat by nightfall. About an hour before sunset, however, with perhaps fifteen miles to go, the hills on either side crowded closer together, squeezing the sky out, the bends be-came tighter and the rapids steeper. I had lost sight of Gerry's craft ahead of me, but after dropping down two sharp rapids that were almost waterfalls, I saw River Rover 01 at the riverside. Gerry had stopped to see if I had been taken by surprise by the last two rapids.

'About half a mile further on, I came upon Gerry again parked on the bank. The water had carved the rock into beautiful but terrible shapes as this great river poured into a bottleneck. Gerry had seen the severe rapid ahead and had stopped to have a closer look from the bank. As we looked at the swirling water, we could see that the river here tumbled through a narrow gorge and over a bed of giant boulders, some submerged and some protruding above the surface. This was the worst rapid we had yet encountered anywhere on the river. Here was a deep foaming vortex — the most formidable feature of white water. While we were mulling over this new difficulty, darkness was fast approaching, so we decided to camp for the night, both to give more time to pick a route through the rapid and to wait for Tony and Stuart following more slowly in Gemini.

'Next morning at about 8 a.m., the Gemini arrived, its crew looking rather wet after tumbling down the last three rapids in a battle to stay with their boat. A few words of explanation, yet another inspection of the next rapid, and we were ready to go, with Ian Stone's camera and Mervyn Broadway's microphone standing by to record whatever might befall us. They were cheerfully prepared to risk life and limb to record our battle.

'The Gemini went down first. The rubber craft was tossed about on the waves; for a moment it reared up at such a crazy angle that I thought it was certain to overturn, but it dropped out of sight into the great hole behind a submerged rock and reappeared the right way up. Seconds later there was a clearly audible crack as the propeller struck a rock and stopped. The paddles instantly appeared in Tony's and Stuart's hands, and the injured Gemini disappeared from sight around the corner with its two very wet crew-men paddling furiously out of the bottom of this giant obstacle.

'Next to go through the hoop was River Rover 01. Gerry spent a few minutes clearing the windscreens, then he climbed into his craft with Doug and Bruce to make his run. He left the sloping beach and turned upriver so that he would have room to get up a little speed. Pulling to the right of the first submerged rock, he made his attempt to turn left, but the force of the water swept him downstream, off the line we had agreed. The hovercraft bucked and yawed through the swirling white water. Gerry seemed to be managing to maintain control, until a loud report and an increase in the engine's pitch signalled some sort of failure. I could not tell exactly what had happened except that the River Rover was hovering with some difficulty through the last stretch of the foaming white water.

'I now boarded River Rover 02 to make my attempt at the treacherous obstacle. I drove down the right-hand side and when we were abeam the first submerged rock I slammed on the full left elevon. I was more fortunate than Gerry, managing to cross the torrent of water and reaching the left-hand edge near a fish-trap. Another maximum effort to turn, this time to the right, brought us round into a down-river direction, so far without any damage. But then we started to go down a series of steps as the water flowed through narrow gaps between rocks. I was able to avoid striking the rocks at either side, but when we were halfway down, the hovercraft ploughed into a hole and a massive wave broke over the bows.

'This would have caused us no problem had not the wave also been breaking over the port side of the craft. The port propulsion fan, which had hitherto been presented only with a spray-filled air to push through its duct, was suddenly immersed in a wall of solid water. With a sharp bang, the nylon fan-blades shattered into tiny pieces under the shock loading and the engines started to emit a high-pitched whine. My craft immediately yawed to the left. With the controls fully deflected to the right, I was almost — but not quite — able to arrest the yaw. In this semi-controlled state we continued down through the narrow gap, until it became obvious that we were going to hit a rock on the left.

'I moved the control column over to the left, arresting the asymmetric thrust, and spun the craft round until we were pointing almost upstream, to reduce the force of the impact. For a second after the starboard side struck the rock we were held against it by the water flow, and I was able briefly to assess what awaited us further down. Having decided on what seemed to be the only possible course of action, I swung the craft quickly to the left into a channel formed by a large craggy rock in midstream. The bows missed the rock by about six inches and we bounced into the maelstrom at the bottom of the rapid in a continuous left turn. An additional vibration audible above the sound of the overspeeding engine signalled damage.

'As we rounded the bend into calmer water, we saw the Gemini and Rover 01 on a tiny beach. Relief flooded through me. Fortunately the beach was on the left bank as that was the only way I could turn. We completed yet another 360° pirouette to the left and finally came to rest within a few feet of the craft resting on the beach.

'We compared notes on our respective experiences. Just as I had lost my port thrust fan, Gerry had lost his starboard. My craft had sustained some slight hull damage, and the extra vibration we had heard turned out to be the result of a missing blade from the lift-fan. This had presumably been broken off by a piece of the shattered thrust blades. However, the major problem in each case was a thrust fan being destroyed by the solid water force of the waves. The descent of the rapid had taken only a few minutes, allowing no time for exhilaration, fear or any other emotion. As in any difficult situation, I was much too busy to have any such feelings.

'Doug Cooledge and Bruce Vincent set to work replacing the missing blades on the two craft. While they were working, Gerry and I walked about a mile down-river, to find out what else the Kali Gandaki had in store for us. After one formidable rapid, not quite as severe as the one we had just negotiated, the river opened out and became calmer and remained so for as far as we could see. When we reached the three craft, we felt able to assure the others that the river should not present any more problems. Our spirits were further raised when a smiling middle-aged man appeared out of nowhere and offered us a bunch of perfectly ripe bananas.

'The fan blades were quickly replaced. For a few seconds or so I hovered to drain water from the rear of the skirt, then I was ready to cross the next formidable rapid. I planned to approach on the right and then cross over the main stream before a great black rock, and continue down the left-hand side. As I turned across the flow, the water caught the craft and despite my attempts to turn left, we were swept to the right and hit the rock with a resounding crash. My shoulder put out a window, and a splintered hole appeared in the side of the hull. With no other damage showing, I continued on down the winding river, using every trick I could think of to stay above hump speed on the bends. River Rover 01, unscathed, passed us on the way at full speed, with friendly waves from its occupants.

'At last, as we rounded yet another bend, there on the beach of Deoghat were our familiar Vango tents. With shouts of elation we hovered over the last half-mile of calm water, and River Rover 02 joined her sister craft on the beach. The following morning, with the minimum of fuss, the two craft swept down four miles of the Narayani river to our down-river target of Narayanghat.

'The events of the waterfall rapids had made me wonder what I was doing putting myself in such situations! But I knew that there was no other hovercraft — indeed no other vehicle — which could have tackled the Kali Gandaki in the way River Rover did. We established the capabilities of the craft, and we also searched out the areas for improvement. River Rover's future is assured. I quietly thanked God for the privilege of being involved in the project.'

We resisted the temptation to explore the wide

stretches of the Narayani river towards the Indian border. This interesting river area open to boats held no special challenge to River Rover.

The town of Narayanghat consisted largely of shacks made of sheeting manufactured for other purposes and often bearing the faded trade name indicating its original use. The wide main thoroughfare was punctuated with pot-holes full of decomposing refuse. These towns of the Terai are magnets to the proud men of the Middle Hills. Until a few years ago, malaria had made the Terai largely uninhabitable but the area now holds out the prospect of an easier life. However, the call to return to the hills was unmistakable to the hovercraft team.

We loaded the Rovers on to lorries, obtained by Paddy's bartering skills, on the east bank of the Narayani river and then both Tata trucks and Rovers were ferried across on an age-old man-powered raft. After a tortuous journey along the East-West Highway across the Terai, then north on the twisting road from Butwal, both craft arrived back at base on 13 February.

Teaming up with our Nepali volunteers of all ages, we heaved the River Rovers off the back of the trucks. Having delivered the craft, one of the elderly Tata trucks refused to start. The Sikh driver borrowed one of our anchor ropes which he proceeded to wind round the half-shaft. He then jacked the back wheels up, lined up our Nepali volunteers at ninety degrees to the truck, laying the rope at their feet just like a tug of war. At a given signal, they picked up the rope facing away from the truck. A shout from the driver and the team ran furiously down the slope. The half-shaft spun and the reluctant engine burst into life!

The hull damage Rover 02 had sustained on the submerged rocks above Deoghat was quickly repaired, thanks to the craft's meccano-type construction, and Rick Elliott's dedicated work. We now set out to operate the craft again on the testing stretches of river north-west of base, where a selection of rapids we had previously graded as severe were now very marginal and potentially dangerous, following a further fall in the water level. I was pleased with our down-river achievements. I was aware that we needed to tread the fine line between pushing River Rover to the absolute limit, and the risk of damage to the craft and danger to the occupants. We would also concentrate on training most of the team to drive over the exacting but exhilarating 'regular route' between base and Camps 1 and 2.

With the BBC's filming complete, we set aside several trips on the spectacular staircase of rapids for photographer Brian Goodwin to make our own film record. He was particularly successful in capturing the technical achievements of the craft and the special driving skills that Gerry and Peter had developed. Brian's film gives an unmistakable answer to the question: 'Just what can your hovercraft do?'

Brian Holdsworth had brought out a secondhand operating table, an X-ray machine, medicines, dressings — and a tennis net for Tansen Hospital, and he deserved the pleasure of personal delivery. The medical supplies and equipment were vital for the ongoing work of the hospital; in its own way, I saw the tennis net as equally needed in providing relaxation for the hard-pressed staff, enabling them to continue their life-saving work.

I was keen to give members of the faithful support team, Brian included, a trek to the high Himalayas. Early on 21 February, seven of us set out from Ramdighat, loaded with trekking kit and compo rations, for Pokhara. Our planned route was from there to Annapurna Sanctuary, the base camp for most Annapurna climbing expeditions. Apart from the experience of living and walking in the high Himalayas and the enjoyment of the majestic mountain scenery, the trek would also allow us to explore the Modi Khola river which rises high on Annapurna and is a main

tributary of the Kali Gandaki. In the event, we could not make it right to the Sanctuary because of deteriorating weather conditions, but our eight days of actual trekking taught us valuable lessons about the geography and the problems of life and travel in this rugged yet colourful part of the world.

It was also time to give the young men their head with Skima 4. This four-seater inflatable hovercraft, manufactured by Pindair Ltd, was purchased primarily as a training vehicle to be carried to isolated sites where River Rover could not go. Its obvious disadvantage was its inability to carry a useful load; in its favour were its lightness and portability, and the fact that its inflatable rubber hull could take a repeated battering in major rapids.

I had disappointed John Rollins by putting the brakes on his ambitious canoeing plans. Neither had he been able to achieve the hovercraft altitude record he'd been hoping for with the Skima 4 on Lake Tilitho, 16,500 feet up in the Annapurna range. However, the improvement of our up-river achievement purely in terms of distance was an ongoing aspiration. So, on 21 February, a four-man party of John, surveyor Dave Porter, Mick Reynolds and Hugh Bennell set off with the Skima, supplies of fuel having been pre-positioned by the River Rover and, further up-river, by porters.

They found that with only one person aboard the hovercraft would go up the most awesome rapids, although by no means easily. The waves were up to eight feet high! For many rapids, they had to spend up to half an hour trying again and again to find a way through; in one case, it took ten attempts before they finally succeeded. The party took turns at driving the craft, not only battling against the river, but also striving to keep the hovercraft serviceable with the limited supply of tools and spares they were carrying. After five days, they had reached a point approximately twenty-two miles up-river from Base Camp. Here they reluctantly turned back, as the constant struggle against rapids had taken its toll.

During these last few days on the river, we also experimented to see if we could charge our radio batteries using the Lucas solar panels. The abundance of sunshine did the job admirably. It gave us a certain satisfaction to obtain 'something for nothing'. But there were more important considerations: loss of battery power and thus use of the radio on an isolated stretch of the river in an emergency could place us in exactly the same position as the sick Nepalis we were seeking to help. The radio link was a life-line. The sunshine was now our stand-by.

Our time on the Kali Gandaki was nearing its end. The talkative priestess of Ramdi invited the team to a Hindu ceremony of thanksgiving for the expedition, to be held in the Ramdighat temple. Although my attitude upset some of the team members, I felt unable to take part in such a ritual. My thanksgiving was directed not to a multiplicity of Hindu deities, but towards the God whom I knew all along had motivated me and been in control of the whole project. It was a lonely and difficult decision, but I could not compromise on this occasion.

Having completed a total of 280 hovering hours and covered approximately 5,200 kilometres, we ceased operations on 5 March 1979. After nearly three months on the riverside we had forged ties of friendship with the Nepali villagers alongside the Kali Gandaki; and we left these friendly people with mixed feelings. The outlook of the team towards the world to which we were returning would be permanently changed.

NINE

NO EASY ANSWERS

With only Paddy Gallacher and two Sherpas left at base for final clearance duties, Bernard Coleman and I made our last journey back to Kathmandu on 7 March in the close confines of the cab of a Tata truck. Our burly Sikh driver was sporting a broad black chin-strap to mark the festival of Red Machendranath. During this month-long festival, red powder is thrown on the fields to ensure that they are well-watered for the coming rice-growing season. Anxious that my fields should be well-watered too, a group of Nepalese threw a cloud of red powder through the open truck window as we bounced along the pot-holed switchback road to Kathmandu.

The Nepalis consider that it is auspicious to plant their rice when this festival is over. Although River Rover has proved to be auspicious for Nepal, we have decided not to leave either craft in the country. The medical mission programme for which the craft was intended is like elastic with all the stretch fully taken up. The available manpower is totally occupied coping with the present task. At Tansen Hospital, three Land Rovers stand unused for shortage of spare parts. It would be most *inauspicious* for River Rover to be the fourth. Lack of a permanent maintenance engineer for continuing operations confirmed this decision.

Yet how vehemently I wished to see our hovercraft in purposeful service in the Fourth World. I was less than enthusiastic about the suggestion that River Rover should give exciting river rides to Western tourists — a suggestion made by influential Nepali officials after a display of the craft's talents at Kathmandu airport.

To the concern and annoyance of the expedition team, River Rover had been the subject of much uninformed cocktail comment amongst the expatriate community in the capital. Whilst I welcomed the opportunity to put the craft through its paces at the airport, the quality of performance on the rapids of the Kali Gandaki was both more impressive and relevant to the needs of Nepal. I had become thoroughly conditioned to unenlightened comments on our project and suggested to the team that the excellent film Brian Goodwin had taken on the wild stretches of the Kali Gandaki coupled with the BBC's *World About Us* report would be the best evidence to answer this uninformed scepticism.

I was disappointed, too, by the fact that the major biennial Services Expedition, which was also an officially recognized research project of the Overseas Development Administration, using a British-built craft of highly innovative design, did not receive any firsthand observation from a responsible British official. The subsequent official report inevitably fell short in the technical understanding of our operations. My report, submitted on return from Nepal, was therefore outranked.

River Rover and the expedition had been an act of faith throughout. Under the pressure of this uninformed comment, a loss of official nerve ensued and much of the positive official Service support evaporated in the final stages of the project. A few faithful supporters in key positions stood by me in these lonely moments. In particular, Squadron Leader Bill Underwood of RAF Movements battled hard to keep the project moving towards its final goal. I knew that members of my home church at Gorsley in Herefordshire took time regularly to pray for the project. During these searching times, I knew that it was only by God's power and strength that I was able to persevere.

Nearly a year later, a Ministry of Defence scientist presented a paper on hovercraft control at the 1980 International Hovercraft Conference, which concluded that the elevon system of our garage-built craft was superior to that used in the Royal Navy's SRN6 hovercraft, built at a cost of hundreds of thousands of pounds of taxpayers' money. Captain Gerry Bradnam, who had driven both the Navy's machines and River Rover, had reached this conclusion after the first launch of 01 on the Kali Gandaki.

Had it all been worthwhile? What had the expedition actually achieved? Must the friendly people we had so briefly helped continue to suffer the ravages of TB, leprosy and other debilitating diseases?

There are no easy answers to the problems of Nepal. For nearly three months we had hovered the rivers and trekked the hills. Just five miles down stream from base, we had come across a loincloth-clad fisherman whose way of life would have been the same centuries ago. We had become hardened to sights of dirt, disease, death and suffering, although it was always something of a shock to find dead bodies on the river — either from the Hindu use of the river for burial or following frequent drownings. The Nepalis are so isolated from sources of help; sometimes if a woman or child is dying, the men show little care because they can always get another wife or conceive another child.

How can we demonstrate to them a Christian standard of love and caring for each person? To show them that they count as individuals is very difficult.

There does seem to be a conflict between the religions of Christianity and Hinduism. Nepal is a Hindu nation, her laws are Hindu, and the caste system forms the backbone of her society. Different caste levels will not even co-operate in a water supply project sharing the same tap. Millions of viewers of the BBC film of the expedition witnessed the tragedy of the emaciated child brought to Robin Dugdale's clinic at Camp 2. The child had been fed with its mother's milk for the first nine months of life. Then another child had come along and the elder one was left to diet on the rice that father brought in from the fields and to drink the contaminated water. At once the child was at risk to all the diseases that are prevalent in a developing country. This poor little fellow had chronic gastro-enteritis and malnutrition which was slowly but certainly sapping the life from his thin, matchstick body. Probably seventy per cent of the adult population are walking around with some kind of intestinal parasite reducing their energy, giving them pain or sucking their blood and making them anaemic. And so we're faced with people whose resistance is low, making them an obvious target for disease and infection. Change is difficult, as most actions have a religious as well as cultural significance. Planting grain in a traditional rice field is feared as it might cause spiritual trouble and a poor crop next season. But it is the lack of adequate communications which is the major obstacle to better health in the villages.

As an expedition, we had had the specific aim of providing a means of transport which could be of lasting value in isolated parts of the Fourth World. We had experienced both adventure and achievement on the Kali Gandaki. We had set out on a demanding, sometimes dangerous, adventure on a fast-flowing, rapid-strewn Himalayan river, using a newly-designed craft of appropriate technology, to bring the possibility of a better quality of life to the people of a remote area.

The Defence Council Instruction asking for projects for consideration for the 9th Sponsored Expedition required an exacting adventure combining scientific or technical value with a high level of public interest. These requirements had been abundantly fulfilled. The project had also been a unique demonstration of inter-Service co-operation, and the inventive skills of the team working on long lines of logistic support were tested to the full.

We reached our target — Narayanghat in the Terai. The two River Rover hovercraft made regular safe shuttle journeys over a sixty-two-mile stretch of a previously unnavigable river in safety over a three-month period. It was the first time that hovercraft had ever climbed rapids of such severity. With the construction of one by-pass around a waterfall, the regular navigable length of river could be increased to sixty-nine miles, thus linking the only two roads in the area. Alternatively, one craft could operate east of the waterfall linking with the other to the west. River Rover proved that a safe long-term operation is possible and established the feasibility of using lightweight hovercraft as a cost-effective means of transport in remote areas of the world. Tested to the limit on additional stretches of water which would never be in regular use, the craft provided valuable technical information for future operations.

Equally important in a developing country is the fact that maintenance of the craft is within the capability of the average handyman and is similar to the servicing of the family car. Running costs are also comparable. Replacing the rubber fingers of the skirt equates to a 25,000-mile tyre-change. As regards the actual handling of the craft, most of the team drove

River Rover over the rapids. The average well-co-ordinated person can quickly learn the rudiments of driving.

The expedition's riverside clinics linked by hover-craft, whilst barely scratching the surface of an immense medical problem, showed that a pilot rural health scheme *could* be serviced by River Rover. In a country as poor as Nepal, it is only the present lament-ably inadequate infrastructure that prevents the establishment of a regular 'hovering doctor service'. Had the United Mission had the capacity to operate River Rover, this service could have gone ahead provided that Nepali government agreement was forthcoming. This piece of appropriate technology could have been put to immediate life-saving use. For the time being, Nepal's priorities are elsewhere. It may be that River Rover came to Nepal five years ahead of its time.

Dr Graham Morris, medical director at Tansen, whose hospital would continue after the River Rovers had gone from Nepal, described his reaction to the expedition after three months of river operations:

'The great rivers of Nepal are for the most part un-navigable because of rapids, broad areas of shallows and torrents in the narrow defiles. For the Nepali a river is something to overcome. You respect it because it belongs to God. All water flows out of the mouth of God and flows back into God. To get your feet in the water just before you die will ensure a comfortable passage into the next incarnation. If you must cross the river you do so with reverence and fear, and with great thankfulness when you reach the other side. You bury your dead in it.

'It was really quite something when we had a hovercraft expedition with the proposal of travelling both down and up the great Kali Gandaki. I was most excited. In the pilot scheme, it was very evident that Mike Cole and his Joint Services team showed that using a hovercraft could make a river in Nepal a high-way instead of an obstacle. What a difference to see these mighty rivers actually used! The expedition planned to service a series of health posts along the river close to the villages, with a medical team travelling the river on the hovercraft providing a mobile clinic with the craft occasionally used as an ambulance.

'This concept does seem feasible to me and they did demonstrate that the craft could be used on this river. I wonder whether a country like Nepal which is now spending large amounts of money building roads might not make more use of its rivers using hovercraft.'

(I was interested to find out that six years' work and many millions of pounds had gone into building ten miles of metalled road (still unfinished) in the middle hills of east Nepal. Our sixty-two miles in four months was express progress by comparison!)

For myself as leader of the expedition to have lasting satisfaction, it was necessary for some permanent progress in hovercraft operations in the Fourth World to result from our efforts. I was encouraged to stick to this aim by officials of both Oxfam and the Save the Children Fund who were enthusiastic about its potential. Paddy Gallacher negotiated to leave River Rover 02 in temporary storage at Kathmandu airport pending its move 'in faith' to some permanent Fourth World location. The balance of equipment, including Rover 01, was prepared for airlift back to the UK.

Up very early on Sunday 25 March, I had the exhilarating experience of attending a service of the Nepali Christian Fellowship in Kathmandu. Sunday is a working day in Nepal, so everything must be concluded in time to start work. I took my boots off at the entrance — my expedition red socks were clearly in need of a darning needle — and sat on the mats to the right; the ladies were all on the left. Nepali Christians are clearly enthusiastic about their faith: they sing with gusto and listen carefully to every word from the preacher. Though I couldn't understand what was being said, I caught the joyful atmosphere of worship. Despite — or perhaps because of — its difficulties, a small, vibrant Nepali church is making a telling impact in a strictly Hindu country.

Confirmation that Ascot Flight 5626 had taken off from Calcutta was the signal for me to seek permission to hover Rover 01 from its helicopter hangar to the dispersal earmarked for our Hercules. Late in the afternoon of Monday 26 March, we heard the familiar roar of four Allison turbo-prop engines and the unmistakable shape of the C130 appeared high over the airport. The loading of our equipment was completed smoothly.

Next day, in the early morning sunshine, we lifted off from Tribhuvan International Airport, locally known as 'the cowfield'. After overnight stops in Muscat and Athens, we touched down at RAF Lyneham in Wiltshire, England, at 6 p.m. on Thursday 29 March. We had missed the arctic weather of the coldest UK winter of the century as well as the discomforts brought about by industrial discontent.

Peter Dixon had prepared a notable homecoming. As well as joyful reunions with our families, we were greeted by representatives of television, radio and the press. I was welcomed back by my wife Jackie — whose radiant Christian faith had supported the project with enthusiasm and prayer right from the outset — and my two children, who seemed so much taller than I remembered them!

On my way home to Linton, our village in Herefordshire, I thought back to a climb I had attempted with Brian Holdsworth just before leaving Nepal. We wanted to reach the 9,200-foot high summit of Phulchonki, from which it is possible to view in one arc the snow-clad Himalayan backdrop from Everest in the east to Dhaulagiri in the west. Our measured pace was too slow and the panorama was partially obscured by the midday heat haze. The promise of the view of Everest could be vaguely sensed — we knew it was there but we couldn't actually see it.

I had left Nepal after nearly four months, having viewed the possibilities of River Rover close at hand. My chief aim was still outstanding — the hovering doctor service was not yet a reality. There was further to go and perhaps I needed to quicken my pace if River Rover was to achieve this objective before the vision faded.

In fact, the summit of the project was still several arduous months away.

TEN

ON ACTIVE SERVICE

The present leadership of the Regions Beyond Missionary Union (RBMU) is in the hands of men with a dynamic, outgoing and pioneering outlook. I had met RBMU Secretary Geoff Larcombe before leaving for Nepal. He had asked me if a craft could be earmarked for use in the wild interior of Irian Jaya in Indonesia if we did not leave it in Nepal. A trained engineer, Paul Kline, with experience on both aircraft and boats was on hand to keep the craft serviceable, and plentiful, cheap petrol was available. Indonesia has its own oil.

Irian Jaya lies within the tropical zone just south of the equator. The main landmass is divided down the centre by a high, mountain range with razor-back ridges and peaks rising to over 16,000 feet. Just four degrees south of the equator there is permanent snow! These jungle-clad mountains form the catchment area for many river systems, both large and small. Much of the country is covered by tropical rain forests rich in animal life. This terrain is among the most isolated and inhospitable in the world. In the interior there are no roads through the mountains and only short, tortuous trails through the jungle. The sprawling archipelago is regarded as a dangerous and primitive area. In the heart of Irian's interior, near the confluence of the Sumo and baliem rivers, the settlement of Sumo consists of a small, wooden 'Robinson Crusoe' house and about fifteen native round, thatched huts, with a narrow grass airstrip cut between the tall jungle trees. The fast-flowing Sumo river is the only route for those who venture into the treacherous jungle to make contact with the tribal people. For several months in the year, the river shrinks to become a maze of narrow rivulets, exposing large sand bars and mud banks. At other times, flash floods produce fast water conditions in a few hours.

At Sumo, Les Henson — missionary, medic and mechanic — and his Dutch wife Wapke, with their baby Joel, are working amongst the Somahai tribe, first discovered by outsiders in 1974. The Hensons seek to heal, educate and counsel some 1,500 Somahai who are scattered in tiny jungle clearings over an area of around 1,250 square miles. Les spends many foot-slogging days trudging out from Sumo to make contact with these people. Having proved its potential in Nepal, River Rover 02 — which we had left in store at Kathmandu Airport — has been earmarked for Les Henson's use on the jungle rivers of Irian Jaya.

Squadron Leader Bill Underwood from his Air Movements desk in the Ministry of Defence had turned up trumps once again. Ascot flight 5756, the May 1979 Hercules global trainer, was routed via Athens, Bahrain, Delhi, Kathmandu, Calcutta, Hong Kong, Sentani (Irian Jaya), Port Moresby (Papua New Guinea), Townsville (Queensland) and then on across the Pacific.

I left home for RAF Lyneham on 14 May. There I met up with the small team of Gerry Bradnam, Bruce Vincent, David Henderson of RBMU and TEAR Fund worker Bernard Coleman, who would be spending several months in remote Sumo, giving a thorough engineering handover to the recipients of River Rover. Waiting to meet us at Lyneham was Paddy Gallacher, who had taken a few days' leave. He checked that our air freight manifests were in order and handed over one more piece of life-saving equipment — a spare part for a Land Rover ambulance at Tansen hospital.

Landing on schedule on 17 May at Kathmandu, I made my way to the control tower. There was a short lull in aircraft movement and we were free to hover Rover 02 from its storage hangar to the mouth of the open rear doors of the parked Hercules. Retired Queen's Gurkha Officer I. B. Gurung kindly loaned his team of wiry Nepali porters to help us manhandle, then lift, load and lash Rover 02 into the aeroplane's empty freight bay. This was hot work, with the afternoon sun reflecting strongly off the tarmac. We rewarded their efforts with a crate of Fanta. I think the porters were hoping it was something stronger!

We deposited our precious medical stores with customs and headed for the United Mission headquarters to alert them to their arrival. There I met pharmacist Paul Spivey. He normally worked at Kathmandu University; however the students were on strike, busily fanning the flames of the latest political issue. They were campaigning for a Western-style democracy to replace the party-less *Panchayat* system introduced under the leadership of the king some eighteen years previously. Shortly after our take-off next day, the students took to the streets of Kathmandu, violently advocating the multi-party system and clashing with anti-riot police. When the issue was later referred to a referendum, the people of Nepal voted to retain the *Panchayat*. King Birenda therefore remains in supreme authority — by the will of the people.

We landed on the runway at Kai Tak at dusk on 18 May after an impressive approach over the towering tenements of Kowloon. A panorama of light reflects from the skyline on to the rain-washed airport apron proclaiming to all the movement, colour and noise which is Hong Kong twenty-four hours a day. No other city so completely combines the material progress of the West with the mystery of the East as does Hong Kong. I was elated at being only seven hours fifty minutes flying time away from Sentani in Irian Jaya, and the achievement of our final goal: River Rover in Fourth World service.

But appreciation of the sights and the anticipation of Rover 02's future were abruptly terminated as I was handed two signals. The first read: 'YOU WILL BE AWARE THAT THERE ARE PROBLEMS OF GAINING LANDING CLEARANCE AT SENTANI FOR DELIVERY OF KALI-CUSHION HOVERCRAFT. DECISION AS TO WHETHER TO PROCEED TO ALTERNATE INDONESIAN AIRFIELD OFFERED MUST BE RESOLVED BETWEEN AIRCRAFT CAPTAIN AND EXPEDITION LEADER IN CONJUNCTION WITH UPAVON HQ 38 GP. HOWEVER, IF IT IS DECIDED THAT DELIVERY TO AN INDONESIAN AIRFIELD IS NOT A FEASIBLE PROPOSITION HOVERCRAFT IS TO BE OFFLOADED IN HONG KONG AS TOTAL AIRCRAFT PAYLOAD IS COMMITTED AUSTRALIA TO U.K.'

The second heralded further problems:

'FOLLOWING IS REPEAT OF MESSAGE RECEIVED FROM BRITISH DEFENCE ATTACHÉ, JAKARTA.

1. GARUDA AIR OPERATORS LOGISTICS BRANCH NOW CONFIRM THAT WEIGHT LIMIT AT SENTANI IS 60,000 POUNDS. RUNWAY ONLY 1,750 METRES LONG. THEY CANNOT REPEAT CANNOT GRANT PERMISSION FOR TASK 5756 TO LAND.

2. BECAUSE OF ADMIN PROBLEMS + EXPENSE OF TRANSFERRING HOVERCRAFT FROM BIAK — RUNWAY LENGTH 3,000 METRES — IF TASK 5756 LANDED THERE INSTEAD, THIS EMBASSY HAS

The stripped-down body of Rover 02 is carried by
helicopter into the heart of Irian Jaya.

SIGNALLED FCO AND MOD(AIR) FOR THEIR ADVICE ON HOW TO PROCEED.

3. REGRET THAT TASK 5756 SHOULD THEREFORE BE POSTPONED PENDING FURTHER INSTRUCTIONS.

4. PARTICULARLY REGRET CONFLICTING ADVICE PREVIOUSLY GIVEN BY INDONESIAN AIR FORCE WHICH HAS RESULTED IN PRESENT SITUATION.

IN VIEW OF ABOVE REQUEST EXPEDITION LEADER ATTEMPTS TO CONTACT BRIT. DEF. ATT. JAKARTA DIRECT IF ANY FURTHER QUERIES SHOULD ARISE. BUT UNLESS THE REQUEST IS MADE BY JAKARTA FOR USE OF ALTERNATIVE AIRFIELD, HOVERCRAFT PLUS PASSENGERS ARE TO BE OFFLOADED IN HONG KONG AND TASK ITINERARY WILL BE REVISED TO DEPART HONG KONG ON ORIGINAL SCHEDULE DIRECT TO PORT MORESBY. REVISED ITINERARY WILL BE ISSUED WHEN THIS MESSAGE ACKNOWLEDGED.'

With landing at Sentani off and take-off for Port Moresby (Papua New Guinea) planned for 9 a.m. on 21 May I had forty-eight hours to retrieve the position. Warming to the aims of our project and to our predicament, Squadron Leader Peter Atkins who was the officer commanding the RAF detachment at Kai Tak, tried everything he could to prevent the River Rover offload. David Henderson and I began a long vigil glued to the telephone and to the airport's teleprinter.

By 4 p.m. on 20 May we had been given clearance for offload facilities at Port Moresby. Two hours later we heard that both of Flight 5756's navigators and the load master had been admitted to hospital with stomach pains and vomiting. Take-off was postponed for forty-eight hours as we awaited the arrival of three replacement crew members from the UK. At breakfast the following morning, Gerry Bradman and Bruce

Vincent also complained of stomach pains and were quickly taken off to hospital.

At the same time officials at Port Moresby informed us that there was no shipping route or overland transportation from Port Moresby to Jayapura (Sentani). They helpfully suggested that we should try to offload River Rover at Wewak airfield in the north of Papua New Guinea. From Wewak it would be possible to ship the craft on to Irian Jaya. By the evening of 21 May clearance had been given for Wewak, but the captain of 5756 had a fuel problem. He needed sufficient fuel overhead at Wewak to allow for a bad weather diversion, but could not be overweight for landing. He agreed to vent some fuel in flight if this proved necessary. Everything seemed set fair for Wewak, and tired but thankful, David, Bernard and I turned in early the night before the final airlift of Rover 02 to New Guinea.

Whilst undertaking his pre-flight checks at Kai Tak airport, the air engineer of Flight 5756 started to vomit. The flight was delayed yet again. Later that day, he was confirmed as having amoebic dysentry. The crew of 5756 plus the hovercraft team would have to be casualty-evacuated back to the UK. Peter Atkins, David Henderson and I had battled long hours for five days and had finally been beaten.

On the morning of 24 May, the rear freight doors of the stranded Hercules opened and I gently hovered Rover 02 past a line of jet aircraft to a storage hangar which, we hoped, would be its home for only a short stay. David Henderson, also still trusting that the hovercraft would soon be on active service in Irian Jaya, cabled the mission staff there to let them know the situation. We seemed so near yet so far. Only seven hours fifty minutes' flying time from our goal, we had aborted and all doors seemed to be closing.

Relaxing at last, I scanned the shipping news in the *South China Morning Post*. My attention was caught by an advertisement placed by the China Navigation Company (CNCO). Every three months, one of their ships plied between Hong Kong and Jayapura. Could this be a way of getting Rover 02 to Irian Jaya now that the unique offer of the global training flight could not be repeated?

That afternoon we crossed on the 'Star' ferry from Kowloon to Hong Kong island to visit the offices of CNCO in Swire House. I wondered if the company was connected in any way with the Swire Group who had been so helpful to the project in its early stages. Mr Daniel Lau, shipping manager of CNCO, furnished us with the forward sailing schedules and a rough estimate of the cost of shipping River Rover to Jayapura.

Next morning I met Peter Atkins at the steps of the special 'CASEVAC' (casualty evacuation) entrance to an RAF VC10 flight bound for the UK. I thanked him warmly for all his efforts on our behalf; he assured me that he would keep an eye on our craft until I could take further action. It was nearly three months later when we were finally able to relieve Peter of his charge.

On 25 July 1959, Sir Christopher Cockerell, John Chaplin and 'Sheepy' Lamb made the unique and somewhat 'hairy' initial hovercraft flight across the English Channel from Dover to Calais in their own creation, the 'SRN1'. In commemoration of this, Alan Bliault, editor of *Air Cushion Review*, and Captain John Lefeaux, Director of British Rail's hovercraft fleet, *Seaspeed*, organized a twentieth-anniversary crossing for lightweight hovercraft, in which River Rover 01 took part. I was joined by Mick Reynolds and Doug Cooledge for this trip.

The busiest waterway in the world is no place to make navigational errors. Captain Derek Meredith had generously invited Mick Reynolds and myself to travel in the crew cabin of his SRN4 on a regular *Seaspeed* return trip to Calais the evening before our crossing. A strong east wind was blowing against the tide and six-foot waves were breaking with some strength against *The Princess Margaret*'s skirts. Mick and I exchanged glances — we didn't need to speak. Returning to Dover at 10 p.m., we could only wait and see. At least we now knew the way!

At 6 a.m. on 25 July 1979, the sky was clear, the wind was a south-westerly, four to seven knots in strength, and the swell was around two feet. Conditions were favourable. Progressing at fifteen knots in good visibility, we kept an eagle eye open for other vessels from our lowly position, a few feet above the surface of the water. Most traffic was passing at ninety degrees to our route on the crowded shipping lanes. The wind freshened but the sea state remained good. The white cliffs of Dover were in our rear view for forty minutes; just fifteen minutes later, we had our first sight of the tall chimney of Calais power station. We reached Calais' jutting breakwater and headed at an exhilarating speed downwind for one mile to Calais Hoverport. We had completed the first ever lightweight hovercraft channel crossing by three people — in a record time of one hour fifty-three minutes! We were greeted by the press, television cameras and refreshments in the VIP lounge, decorated with British and French flags. How delicious to taste fresh croissants and French coffee!

Mick and I planned to carry on down the French coast to Boulogne while Doug took the support vehicle by road. Just as Mick Reynolds and I were about to head out from Calais, a single-seat Kestrel GT sport hovercraft arrived, having crossed from Dover in one hour thirty-seven minutes. Our record was short-lived! We met fairly choppy water around Cap Gris Nez as the wind stiffened and the swell rose to four or five feet.

Coming ashore at Boulogne, we found that we had posed the coastguard a real problem. There is no classification for lightweight hovercraft in French maritime regulations. It was too small at eight metres long to be a hovercraft; it ought to have been classed as a rowing boat, but that obviously wasn't right. Was the craft registered? Where were our driving licences? Surely we had a certificate of construction on board? I was beginning to get exasperated with all this. 'I don't know about that, but I should think it's pretty sound,' I assured him. 'It's been up the Himalayas you know.' Collapse of French coastguard!

Early next morning, we lifted River Rover onto its road trailer ready for the journey to Paris. River Rover on the Seine was due to appear on French television that evening. Twenty kilometres from Paris we were met by an escort of police motor-cycle outriders. We were whisked to the banks of the Seine — through twenty sets of red traffic lights! Other traffic was pushed aside to allow 'la petite aeroglisseur' to keep its appointment.

In Nepal, Mick Reynolds had developed a talent for driving the hovercraft with some flair. Paris demanded a showman — and Mick's handling of Rover under the bridges of Paris was as eye-catching to the afternoon riverside promenaders as it was later that evening on television screens all over France. In the still air, Rover 01 leapt over hump and quickly reached forty knots. I wondered what the speed limit was. I felt certain it would only apply to boats after our experience in Boulogne! For the benefit of the cameras we made several passes at speed by the foot of the Eiffel Tower.

We had come to Paris to say thank you to Renault, the main sponsors of the Nepal expedition. The craft was parked for five days in a place of honour — outside the Renault Restaurant in the Champs Elysées — to attract the admiring gaze of the Parisians. Next to it was a large billboard proclaiming in French the achievements of River Rover in Nepal and on the Channel. From this I couldn't quite make out whether the craft was of French or British origin!

We planned to hover River Rover into the hold of *Seaspeed*'s SRN4 *Princess Margaret* hovercraft for the return journey from Calais to Dover. At the height of the busy holiday travel season, this was to be done on the last crossing of the evening. With cars, caravans, coaches and River Rover safely aboard, the *Seaspeed* craft was ready to leave for Dover but the engine on the rear loading ramp wouldn't start, so the sea doors could not be closed. After an hour no progress had been made. The Calais terminal booking clerks made enquiries, seeking 400 beds for the night.

The captain asked our REME engineer Mick Reynolds to have a look. Drawing on his experience of many such situations with stranded Army vehicles, Mick checked the fuel. Why was there petrol in a diesel engine? Within half an hour Mick had drained off the offending fuel, and the engine sprung into life. His skills had proved as effective on the world's premier passenger hovercraft as on the remote river banks of Nepal, and he had also saved *Seaspeed* a sizeable overnight accommodation bill!

We were obviously pleased to have achieved the Channel crossing and had enjoyed our experience on the River Seine — but River Rover 02 remained in store in Hong Kong and our final goal of in-service operation in the Fourth World was still unfulfilled.

I had discovered that the China Navigation Company was indeed part of the Swire Group who had supported the expedition so nobly from the outset. So I wrote to Duncan Bluck, Swire's Deputy Chairman in Hong Kong, seeking his assistance in shipping River Rover to Jayapura. I also asked if the three-man handover team could be passengers on the ship. Swire's

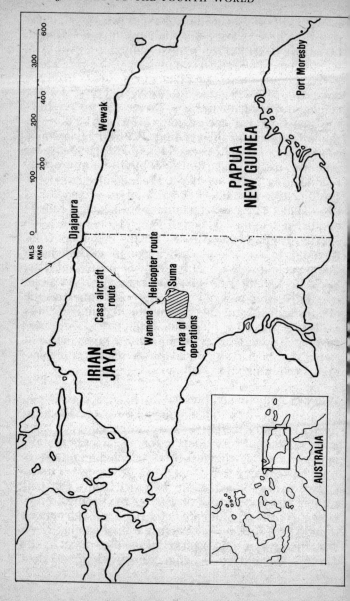

reply was both generous and total: River Rover was granted a free bill of lading and could travel as deck cargo on board CNCO ship *Hupeh* sailing to Jayapura on 22 August, and the three-man delivery team were to be given free return air tickets Hong Kong to Papua New Guinea with Cathay Pacific Airways.

The success of the River Rover craft in the demanding situations of Nepal had been made possible through the driving techniques carefully developed on the rapid-strewn river, combined with the regular and thorough maintenance carried out by our engineers. I was keen that the handover to RBMU in Irian Jaya should include the passing on of as much of our accumulated expertise as possible. One craft in productive service and kept going for many years in the Fourth World would be worth many craft discarded after a few months. All the Service team members were now back at their primary tasks. Was there anyone with the necessary experience available?

Ed Chase grasped the nettle, and took a notable step of faith. He resigned from a well-paid job as an engineer for Plessey to team up with Bernard Coleman and David Henderson of RBMU to deliver Rover 02 to its destination. On Tuesday 14 August 1979, Ed, Bernard and David left Heathrow Airport for Hong Kong.

But it seemed that things were not destined to go smoothly this time either. Ten days later, the August Bank Holiday was about to begin. I received a signal from Bernard Coleman in Hong Kong: 'MAJOR CRISIS HAS ARISEN REGARDING "RIVER ROVER" TRANSPORTATION TO SWIRE SHIP. MAIN PROBLEM IS BANK HOLIDAY WEEKEND 25 AUG — 27 AUG INCLUSIVE. NO TRANSPORT CRANE OR LANDING CRAFT AVAILABLE DUE TO THIS. LOADING TIME FOR SHIP P.M. MONDAY 27 AUG. DEPARTING 28 08.00. CIVILIAN POLICE ESCORT FOR WIDE LOAD UNAVAILABLE FOR REASON OF HOLIDAY ALSO. CIVILIAN TRANSPORTATION APPROACHED AL-

THOUGH POLICE UNAVAILABILITY STILL APPLIES AND THEY QUOTE £100 FOR LIGHTER AND THE SAME FOR ROAD MOVE. NEXT SHIP DUE LATE OCT SENTANI DESTINATION. SUGGESTION FOR FURTHER ACTION APPRECIATED.'

The *Hupeh*, which had been due to sail for Hong Kong on 22 August, had been delayed by a typhoon in the South China Sea. It would now arrive, unload, load and depart over the holiday weekend. With River Rover isolated in storage, Bernard was cabling me for advice. Apart from an improbable idea of driving River Rover across the apron at Kai Tak airport, off the side of the runway protruding into Victoria harbour and then across the water to rendezvous with the *Hupeh* at anchor off Stonecutters Island, I had little of practical use to offer. I could only pray that the sailing of the *Hupeh* would somehow be delayed for at least twenty-four hours until the holiday was over.

A cautious but optimistic signal received on 28 August indicated that SS *Hupeh* departure for Hong Kong had been delayed. The final joyful confirmation arrived from Bernard the next day: 'RIVER ROVER NOW LOADED ON VESSEL. EVERYTHING SHIP-SHAPE. COLEMAN IN HIGH SPIRITS.' I acknowledged my thanks to Squadron Leader Peter Atkins and his staff at Kai Tak who had given Bernard such whole-hearted support in these testing moments. I knew that they shared the vision of the project's potential. At 4 p.m. on Tuesday 28 August, under the watching eyes of many Vietnamese boat people lining other ships anchored nearby, River Rover was hoisted from a borrowed land craft onto the decks of the *Hupeh*. It left at first light the following morning, after a delay of twenty-four hours — just long enough. My prayer had been answered.

Ed Chase takes up the story of the last leg of the eventful journey:

'It was quite a day when the *Hupeh* docked at

Jayapura on 6 September with its unusual deck cargo. The bystanders were curious, the customs officials unsure whether to classify this strange vehicle as a car, boat or aeroplane — after all, it had some functions of all three. The tussle started to get River Rover released from customs. (The pessimists had told us that this process could take three months.) "Of course it's a car," they said. "We saw you drive it up the quay after it was unloaded from the ship. That will be 200 per cent duty." "Ah, but it will spend most of its life on a river, so it must be a boat," we replied, hoping for the 25 per cent duty payable on boats.

'The situation after nearly two weeks of negotiation was stalemate. Then I remembered having read somewhere that a Skima 4 inflatable hovercraft had been imported into Irian a few years before. Paul Kline, RBMU's roving engineer who was taking over maintenance responsibility for River Rover, searched the files for the relevant papers and was delighted to see that the Skima 4 had been categorized as a boat. He took the papers along to the customs office. After a few nail-biting minutes they said, "Well of course, if that one was allowed in as a boat we shall do the same with this. You can take your craft away from the customs shed tomorrow."

'After only fourteen days, Rover 02 was on its way again to the tiny grass airstrip at Sumo in the heart of Irian's jungle interior. It made the journey from the waterfront to the Mission Aviation Fellowship (MAF) base at Sentani on a wide-bodied truck. Its arrival was a special event for the folk there, not least for the children who came and inspected this new vehicle. On the runway, River Rover demonstrated its ability to cope with the land and other obstacles, and we gave rides to MAF folk and others who had helped us to get this far.

'MAF had made hangar space available for Bernard and me to strip River Rover ready for this final stage.

The craft had been designed for such occasions: making full use of its simple *meccano*-type construction, we cut its width down to fit inside a small, square-bodied Cassa transport plane (about half the size of a Hercules) which we had chartered locally to take the craft to Wamera, halfway to Sumo. We shouldered Rover 02 into the cargo hold with only one inch to spare at the side and three inches above.

'The interior of the country was so different from the area around the capital, Jayapura, that it felt like stepping into a time machine and going back into the Stone Age. After droning over 150 miles of solid jungle and winding rivers, we landed at Wamera in the highlands of Irian. Discounting the heat and dense forest, the terrain reminded me of Nepal. The typical Third World concrete houses in Wamera looked familiar too, but it was worth pausing to consider that every bag of cement and every sheet of corrugated aluminium had been airlifted in, as there was no road on which to transport supplies.

'The crowd gathered at the airport watching us were from the Dani tribe. Most of them wore their traditional dress: a string "mini-skirt" for the women and a long thin gourd for the men. On the higher mountains, the Irianese live in sub-zero temperatures dressed like this. Even at Wamera's 5,000-foot altitude, I felt chilly without a sweater.

'The only practical way to get River Rover to Sumo was to airlift it over the high mountain range. A reconnaissance trip had been made by helicopter to see if the only alternate route — up the Baliem River — could be used. At first, the river was well within the scope of the Rover. But, on entering the 9,000-foot mountain range, it flowed through a seven-mile gorge, which presented a real hazard for any water craft. More important, the steep sides prevented the stops along the way which we needed in order to take a breather and plan each stage at a time. To attempt a seven-mile staircase stretch of boulder-strewn rapids at one go would have put the vehicle at high risk and could have proved fatal to the crew. The only way forward was "up and over".

'The whole project had started in 1970 with MAF(UK). MAF(USA) were now to make a momentous contribution for the final push to the goal. Another "first" was about to be clocked up: River Rover would fly over the massive eastern mountain range suspended beneath their Hughes 500 helicopter. Irian Jaya is regarded by pilots worldwide to be one of the most dangerous areas for flying light aircraft, with its hazards of high mountains and dense jungles. But the dedicated and skillful MAF pilots fly daily across these vast areas of primitive uncharted land relying on visual contact, for there are no sophisticated navigational aids here.

'As the grass airstrip at Sumo was too short, narrow and soft to take planes big enough to carry a dismantled River Rover, RBMU had decided that the only way to fly her in was to dangle her below a helicopter. MAF's five seater Hughes 500 helicopter had a lifting capacity of only 800 pounds; Rover's hull weighed 825 pounds, so every removable item was taken off the helicopter — the doors, passenger seats, emergency equipment — to increase its carrying capacity. Ropes were attached to the rear of the hull. Experienced, pioneering pilot Larry Ayott took off and hovered right over Rover 02 whilst two of us attached the ropes to the hook underneath the chopper. We put a swivel by the hook to allow River Rover to turn without tangling the ropes. The downwash from the rotor blades five feet above us tugged at our clothing.

'Slowly Larry increased altitude and the ropes tightened. I checked that they were not tangled and Larry applied more power. The rear of the hovercraft lifted off the ground. Seconds later, she was standing on her nose with her stern in the air. Squeezing the last few horsepower from the Hughes' engine, Larry lifted her clear and slowly flew forward and upward into the distance.

'Once he was out of sight, we could only follow his progress from his occasional radio calls. The static, the suspense and the American accents made these sound like a NASA moon landing. The drag caused by River Rover was so great that the chopper's normal 130-knot top speed was severely cut. Larry reported that he was only reading forty-three knots. One mile out of Wamera, things started to go badly wrong. The slip-stream whistling past the dangling Rover caused it to start swinging like a pendulum and then to spin round and round. The helicopter began to sway drunkenly around the sky. Every swing of the pendulum had to be compensated for by drastic movements of the chopper's controls. The situation was so bad that Larry couldn't even turn round to come back. His thumb edged towards the little red button on the end of the joystick which could eject the ropes from the hook, sending the Rover 02 crashing 200 feet down to the ground.

'By now Larry had discovered how to counteract the swinging but the spinning had become very fast at one revolution every two seconds. His thumb edged back from the button and he brought the chopper round to return to Wamera. His 500 hours of sling-load work in helicopters were proving their worth! Slowly he came back to the landing pad and lowered the still fast-spinning hull. I rushed forward to stop the spinning before Larry let it touch the ground. For a few seconds I stood below the wildly revolving craft towering eighteen feet above me, wondering how to stop it. Then I grasped it in both hands and was nearly knocked off my feet. It was like jumping onto a moving train.

'With the spinning stopped, Larry gently lowered

it to the ground and we all breathed a sigh of relief. The craft hadn't got any nearer Sumo but at least it was undamaged. We made two more attempts to lift it that afternoon, first without the swivel and then slung horizontally instead of vertically, but the results were only worse. Fifty miles short of the target we were stuck. I went to sit down in one of the MAF pilot's houses. On the wall was the text, "They that wait on the Lord shall renew their strength, they shall mount up with wings as eagles". I thought how appropriate the promise was for us at that particular moment. We certainly needed renewed strength from God to help us to carry on despite the setbacks.

'That evening we came to the conclusion that the only thing to hold the craft in a straight line would be a drogue-type parachute like fighter planes string out from the tail when they land on short runways. One of the MAF pilots remembered that there was an old ordinary 'chute in the hangar store — a little moth-eaten when examined, but fine silk, and proudly stamped "Pioneer Parachutes Ltd 1942"! The better segments were used to form a six foot 'cone' with a hole in the tapered end. It was zigzag-stitched on the pilot's wife's machine, and we then completed it with a wire hoop and ties, attaching it to a heavy swivel so that it wouldn't get fouled up in the tail rotor.

'Next day, the 6th of October, we prepared to try it out. The extra drag of the drogue meant that the helicopter couldn't lift off without using more power than was safe, so a few gallons of fuel were offloaded. Larry would have to refuel at the mission airstrip at Holowon. The drogue was laid out behind the helicopter and Larry slowly eased his way upwards. To everyone's delight the drogue worked, though Larry was certainly busy at the controls, and I watched anxiously through binoculars until he was out of sight. At Sumo, the Somahai people became very excited when they saw this strange flying machine appear over the trees. Never had they seen such a sight before. Not many Westerners had seen flying like this either!'

The next stage of the operation is described by Bernard Coleman:

'Following the spectacular airlift of the craft, the second helicopter load consisted of the Rover's eighteen-foot long sidedecks. They overhung at either side of the fuselage, transforming the rotary-wing machine into something resembling an autogyro. Larry, Ed and I climbed in. This was my first helicopter ride — and an exciting one to say the least, for when we were flying through the mountains, gusts of wind tried to swing the helicopter with its protruding load. Within minutes we had left behind the Baliem gorge and were heading for Sumo, which lay somewhere in the vast expanse of rain forest. From our lofty perch, we could see what appeared to be a "tight cauliflower" jungle, broken only by the twisting river. It was exciting to realize that these breaks in the forest cover were to become "roads" for Les Henson in River Rover.

'We turned tightly over a small clearing. There was a single aluminium-roofed shack at the end of a grass airstrip, and a few thatched huts. The helicopter descended rapidly to Sumo. The heat and humidity here were almost overwhelming. Greetings were exchanged with Les and Wapke Henson while their baby son Joel, stared at us curiously. We entered the Hensons' sparsely furnished home for a welcome cup of tea plus a snack for Larry Ayott, today's hero. The house was of simple construction; constant noise emanated from the walls as the insects chewed their way through. An untreated wall lasts eighteen months. We didn't fare much better ourselves, being persistently attacked by mosquitoes. Ed ended up with malaria.

'The Somahai crocodile hunters, hearing that a strange

Guided by local helpers, Rover 02 makes its way to
the river at Sumo – on active service at last.

new river boat was coming, had thoughtfully built a "garage" for River Rover from jungle materials. It took just three days for the hovercraft, now renamed "Regions Rover", to be assembled in the relative cool of this new garage. Once it had been reconstructed, a land test-run was made on the grass airstrip to ensure that belts and fans were lined up correctly. This also allowed Les Henson to be introduced to his new craft. Apart from gently sliding down the slope on the runway and ending up in someone's vegetable garden, Les's first trip went well. All the hovercraft parts seemed to be in good working order, and Les had ten minutes driving experience under his belt!

'With Les Henson's help, Sumo is becoming a village centre for the Somahai tribe. This area of jungle has until very recently been untouched by Western civilization and inter-tribal feuds spelt danger for foreigners. Many of the men at Sumo have killed at least once, some several times. It was in 1977 that Les arrived and persuaded these people to stop killing their enemies in other tribes. Now the men no longer wear their warrior decorations and are usually at peace. Many Somahais still wear other bodily decorations — pieces of bone and large thorns through their noses, believing that these adornments will keep away evil spirits.

'The Somahai have yet to see a wheeled land vehicle as it is impossible to get a Land Rover across the highlands and through the jungle. But they were familiar with the helicopter and Britten Norman Islander aircraft which could land at Sumo. The Regions Rover was therefore accepted very quickly by the villagers as a normal kind of vehicle to be brought in by these friendly strangers. It contrasted vividly with the log dug-out canoes which their own fishermen poled along the stretches of Sumo River when water conditions allowed. In this area, the river alternated between a fast-flowing torrent and a meagre trickle of water. We were confident that Regions Rover would cope with the fast wide river, treacherous rapids, sandbars and mud banks, and also be able to "short circuit" many of the large bends, cross swamps and uncovered river beds. Skimming along on its cushion of air, Regions Rover would seek to build its own highway during all states of the river to reach the widely scattered and isolated Somahais with life-saving medical help.

'Regions Rover was introduced to Irian Jaya rivers on 11 October as we set out upstream on the Sumo. Les picked up the essentials of driving after only two hours' instruction, no doubt helped by his knowledge of the river from many treks. We also made a sortie downriver to reconnoitre the volume of water with the dry season approaching, and also to mark the location of dead trees which had been swept into the river when it was in spate.

'Les had heard that a hunting party were several miles downriver and he was hoping to make contact. After travelling for half an hour, without seeing any signs of human activity, we spotted a small dug-out canoe on the bank, and Les nosed the Rover towards it. As he stepped ashore, a small party of men came out from behind the trees to meet him. Several of them embraced him warmly for it turned out that he had met a number of them sometime back at Sumo. The others were meeting an outsider for the very first time.

'Growing in confidence we ventured further from base on longer trips, making new contacts and holding clinics. We explored the Baliem River, and were offered turtle eggs by local hunters. Their primitive thatched huts, hidden in the dense forest, were impossible to see from our landing point a few yards away. Some of the people along this river rated treachery as the greatest virtue; on hearing the Christian gospel for the first time, they had regarded Judas Iscariot's betrayal of Christ as the act of a hero!

'We planned a two-day venture to hover still further down the Baliem River. Getting quickly over hump, we were doing well. Les, in the driving seat, took a prolonged look at some folk on a large sand-bar island and hit a dead tree which swiped the fan guard. We got to a sand-bar to check the damage just in time to see a rubber drive-belt part. I reached for the spares box, confident that replacement would only take about fifteen minutes, but there were no spare belts — we had failed our pre-flight checks. We had to walk and wade to a settlement three miles downriver.

'We inflated our life-jackets. Even roped together, we had a "hairy" crossing due to the river's strong current. Our feet only occasionally touched a high mound of sand. Knowing that there were crocodiles in the river made us less inclined to dither! The walking was through nearly impenetrable jungle. On reaching the settlement, we dispatched a runner to Sumo with a note for Ed. He returned in the evening with the belts, and I fitted them first thing the next morning. We had been reminded of a serious lesson — thankfully fairly painlessly — and we hovered gratefully back to base.

'I continued my handover task until returning home on 26 January 1980. It was tremendous to be able to see the potential of the hovering clinic service, which Les would be able to undertake. Lives could be saved and new settlements reached. These isolated people would be able to receive the medical help and counsel for which they had waited such a long time. Les Henson's mechanical skills and Paul Kline's maintenance programme for Rover 02 should ensure the long-term operation of the craft.'

With three months of productive operations completed, David Martin, field director of RBMU, wrote telling me about his journey aboard Regions Rover:

'The Rover is an amazing vehicle. At the present time, use of a conventional boat is out of the question here and the hovercraft performs so well. There are many shallow areas and sections of the river full of submerged logs but the craft takes them all in its stride.

'Les made an excellent job of driving the craft. We journeyed from Sumo beyond the convergence with the Baliem River seeking the Poroate and Indama groups. This trip convinced me of the suitability of the craft for the task. About forty minutes after leaving Sumo we came to where a canoe was pulled onto a mud bank. Unfortunately the occupants had left, probably to hunt wild pig. Later we returned past this point, but the canoe had gone. This impressed upon me some of the difficulties the Hensons face in making regular contact with these semi-nomadic people. If he can have a radio installed to keep him in touch with base, Les is hopeful of taking Rover on even longer journeys to other scattered Somahai settlements further west.'

On 1 April 1980, I received a letter from Les Henson at Sumo. Regions Rover was going well, even though termites were attacking the battery! Many trips had been made and several new groups contacted. The crocodile hunters had provided two drums of petrol as a thanks offering for the craft. Les also thanked me for a gift for the radio. I had mentioned how useful a radio would be during an evening expedition lecture in the Midlands. An anonymous listener that night had provided one.

The aims of expeditions supported by the Joint Services Expedition Trust are:

1. to provide a testing adventure;
2. to have technical or scientific content;
3. to be of wide interest to the public.

In so many and varied ways, these aims had been more than fulfilled.

In a thoughtful moment, I had listed additional desirable ingredients for Exercise Kali-Cushion:

1. the coherent pursuit of a goal;

2. an oportunity for self-expression and development of the creative talents of team members;

3. the taking of calculated and meaningful risks;

4. the development of a selfless care for the needy we were certain to meet.

I had condensed these ideas into a single additional aim, based on the challenge that Dr Bill Gould had given to me in 1975: that the expedition should be of lasting value to the Fourth World — that the hovering doctor service should become a reality.

I had pursued this additional aim with a tenacity which others might well have labelled obstinacy or fanaticism. However, I was prepared to walk in the loneliness of my own convictions. The British Services have a fine record of good works in the Fourth World, but I had taken Kali-Cushion a stage further through my association with life-saving agencies which were also Christian missions. To have a link, albeit tenuous, between an official Services' project and Christian mission certainly was the cause for concern, in some quarters. For my part, I am truly grateful to the Royal Air Force for giving me the opportunity of a lifetime to lead the expedition.

The Joint Services Expedition Trust rightly sets great store on the support of the Royal Geographical Society (RGS) for major service adventures, and the Society had supported our expedition. The RGS was founded 150 years ago on the wave of public interest in the exploration of the great African rivers — the Nile, the Zambezi, the Congo and the Niger. Famous explorers such as Samuel Baker and David Livingstone also caught the imagination of that age. They had sought to open up these great water-courses as routes for medicine and for mission, as well as seeking the abolition of slavery through a combination of trade and Christianity.

The inventions of this century, such as the hovercraft, also have a part to play in the future exploration of the great river routes of the world and the setting up of regular communication links. River Rover 01 refurbished has now been earmarked for medical use on the Rio Apurimac in the high Andes of Peru. And in 1982 two new River Rovers will set out on another major expedition — to travel the 3,400 miles from the mouth to the source of the mighty Yangtze Kiang river in China. That could well start a new chapter of events with as many variations as the Kali Gandaki itself.

I can't help thinking that Livingstone, 'the great doctor of Africa', would have thoroughly approved of the hovering doctor service. Our modest attempt to follow in the pioneering spirit of these founders of modern exploration was not without cost. 'Journey to the Fourth World' was only possible because so many people gave what they could to the project in the situation in which they found themselves, whether time, skills, energy or money. Men and women, team members and many supporters, had given in the same spirit as the boy who gave his loaves and fishes to Jesus for him to use to feed 5,000 people. For us, as for them, the power of God had performed the miracle.

Appendix A

Appraisal

Tony Burgess (Manager for Technical Development,
RFO Inflatables Ltd)

*Tony Burgess trained as an engineer in the aircraft industry
before joining the Scientific Civil Service on the Government's
Hovercraft R and D programme, working first at the Royal
Aircraft Establishment and then at the MOD Inter-Service
Hovercraft Unit (IHU). Within IHU he participated in many
trials, including those with the fifty-five ton BH7 Hovercraft
in Sweden and USA. In his spare time he helped Tim Longley
with the design of the MAF 'Missionnaire' hovercraft; this
included the design of the flexible skirt for which he
developed a new simplified production method. He is now
technical development manager of RFD Inflatables Ltd.*

I believe history may well show the Joint Services
Hovercraft Expedition to Nepal to have been an important
watershed in the unfolding story of the use of hovercraft
amongst the nations of the world. Commercial interests
and technical perseverence have brought them into
regular passenger vehicle ferry service. The dictates of
defence policy have brought them into military, naval and
coastguard use around the world. And although they had
been used in the developing nations before the expedition
— generally for scientific purposes — to my knowledge
none had previously been introduced with totally
humanitarian aims.

Dr Bill Gould's vision for the hovercraft equivalent of
the flying doctor service on the rivers of Nepal was a truly
noble one. To be present among these dignified if
materially poor people, to realize that even with plaster
and ointment in one's pocket one could attend to some of
their day-to-day medical needs, was to have the validity of
that vision confirmed in one's own experience. The
expedition showed that such a vision can be turned into
reality. A hovercraft *can* serve the development needs of
riverside village communities. Perhaps for Nepal it is not

yet opportune, as the country's desperately limited resources find other priorities for their attention.

The practicability, then, has been demonstrated. That in itself could be considered ample reward for the hours of labour, the exercise of planning and faith that went into the expedition's preparation and fulfilment. But there is a greater reward still, as Rover 02 operates on the jungle rivers of isolated inland Irian Jaya in the hands of the missionaries there. Its continuing service underlines this fact that a hovercraft of simple design can serve minority groups in a developing nation's hinterland. Long may it serve usefully.

My own part was a small one, but in six months it provided some experiences which must surely remain unforgettable. I look back on my involvement with a sense of privilege, a sense of having done something very worthwhile, a sense of having been close to history in the making.

What's so special about River Rover

Tim Longley, designer

Born in the Seychelles Islands, Tim Longley spent his childhood in Aden, Malta and Portugal. After secondary schooling in England, he began a career in aircraft design at the de Havilland Aeronautical Technical School, with apprenticeship at the de Havilland Aircraft Company, Hatfield. There he lead a group of apprentices who built a Druine 'Turbi' two-seat light aircraft as a private venture. After completion of five years apprenticeship, he spent two years on the design staff of de Havilland, working on the Comet 4 and Trident airliners. On call-up for National Service he joined the Army for a three-year Short Service Commission in the Royal Electrical and Mechanical Engineers. He was posted to Malaya as second-in-command of an Army Air Corps Squadron workshop; while there he learnt to fly. Later, after leaving the Army, he obtained a Commercial Pilot's Licence and spent one year in Australia flying as a Charter Pilot. On return to UK he obtained his aircraft maintenance engineer's licences and joined Missionary Aviation Fellowship as engineer for the newly-established flying programme in the Republic of Chad, Central Africa. Through this experience of operating boats and amphibious aircraft on Lake Chad he became interested in the possibilities of using small hovercraft. Because no suitable commercially-produced hovercraft was available, Tim, together with Tony Burgess, became involved in a design of their own, which eventually took shape as the 'Missionnaire'.

This appendix is intended to cater for those who wish to delve more deeply into the technicalities of River Rover. In particular, the 'elevon' control system is explained in some detail. First, however, some of the basic problems facing any hovercraft designer are discussed. An understanding of these problems will help the reader to appreciate more readily the value of some of the innovations introduced on the River Rover.

The 'hump' problem

Every schoolboy is familiar with Archimedes' Principle, which states that, when a body is wholly or partially immersed in a liquid, it experiences an upthrust equal to the weight of liquid it displaces. It may not, however, be immediately apparent that a hovercraft, which is not immersed in the water at all, nevertheless conforms to Archimedes' Principle.

When a hovercraft is hovering stationary over the water, the lift force due to the pressure of the supporting cushion of air exerts an equal and opposite force on the water beneath the craft. In so doing, it forms a trough in the water. The weight of water displaced by this trough is exactly equal to the all-up weight of the hovercraft.

If the craft now begins to move forward, this trough moves with it, and a bow wave, or 'hump' begins to heap up just ahead of the craft. As speed increases, so the size of the wave increases. Before the hovercraft can reach a speed where it is able to skim, or 'hydroplane', over the surface of the water, it must have the power to ride up and over its own bow wave. This process is known as 'getting over hump', and the speed at which it occurs is known as the 'hump speed'. On River Rover, hump speed varies between about six knots for a lightly-loaded craft, and about ten knots at maximum all-up weight. The power required to get over hump at these speeds is approximately double that required to maintain a cruising speed of twenty-five knots under calm conditions. The hovercraft designer is thus faced with a further problem.

The power problem

In choosing an engine to power his craft, the designer finds himself on the horns of a dilemma. On the one hand, he must avoid installing an engine which is not powerful enough to accelerate the craft through hump speed under the operational conditions expected. On the other hand, he must not sacrifice economy of operation by installing an engine which is excessively large and heavy. Such an engine would inevitably have a higher fuel consumption, so that a greater weight of fuel would need to be carried to achieve a given range. Thus the benefits of higher power could be more than cancelled out, and the lighter, less powerful engine prove to be the best solution.

In Nepal, it was felt that the River Rover could have benefitted from having a more powerful engine, to enable it to overcome some of the more severe rapids. As a rule, only three of the craft's six seats could be filled when travelling upstream for any great distance. In Irian Jaya, however, where river conditions are less extreme, the complaint seems to be that River Rover's cabin is not big enough to take more than seven people at a time! Short of designing a larger, more powerful, less economical craft, little more can be done to help our friends in Irian Jaya. However, future craft will have the more powerful 2000cc engine. This will greatly improve performance under extreme conditions, such as those experienced in Nepal, without increasing fuel consumption much above the present figure of two and a half gallons per hour.

Apart from the design considerations we have discussed, it can also be seen that, for economical operation, it is most important for a hovercraft pilot to keep his craft above hump speed as much as possible. Unfortunately, the moment he gets over hump, he exchanges one problem for another:

The control problem

We in MAF first experienced this problem with the Missionnaire hovercraft, which we designed and built for use on the shallow waters of Lake Chad in Central Africa. This craft earned an enviable reputation for itself in terms of performance and mechanical reliability. In July 1975 it established a record for light hovercraft by circumnavigating the Isle of Wight in two hours fourteen minutes — a distance of sixty nautical miles. Attempts to better this time have been made by other craft, but, as far as is known, this record still stands.

In spite of these successes, the Missionnaire was never sent to Lake Chad. Such was the effect of several years of drought, that a hovercraft was no longer needed. Where previously the missionary doctor had used a motor launch,

Land Rovers were now being used on the dry bed of the lake! Another missionary doctor, Dr Bill Gould in Nepal, asked whether the Missionnaire could be used instead on the winding, rapid-strewn Kali Gandaki.

After due consideration, we had reluctantly to refuse this request. The Missionnaire had been designed for the wide open spaces of Lake Chad, and for this its control system was perfectly adequate. The exacting and potentially dangerous conditions on the river in Nepal demanded a radically new approach to the problem of providing better control. Such conditions dictated a number of new design considerations, the most important being that a suitable hovercraft should be able to make relatively tight turns with the minimum of the sideways skidding which is normally associated with hovercraft planing on the water above hump speed.

Work was begun on a totally new design. This became known in its early stages as the 'Hump'. Apart from its general hovercraft connotations, this stood for 'Hovercraft, Utility, Multi-Purpose'. This craft was to be the forerunner of the River Rover. Attention was focused on ways of using the energy of the air accelerated by the propulsion propeller to do the work of banking the craft. On the Missionnaire, with its large fin and rudder located just behind the propeller, the rudder was sufficiently powerful to impart an appreciable amount of rolling motion to the craft. This 'rudder-induced roll' is for the most part, though not always, of a counter-productive nature. Figure 1 shows how it has the undesirable effect of making the craft roll outwards in a turn. The solution of the problem seemed to lie in using horizontally-hinged control surfaces with a function similar to that of ailerons on an aircraft. By placing them in the slipstream of the two propulsion fans located on either side of the craft's centre line, as far outboard as possible, a fairly powerful rolling moment could be achieved when the control surfaces were deflected differentially. With little extra complication it would be possible for the two control surfaces to be deflected simultaneously in the same direction. They would thus combine the functions of both ailerons and elevators, to use the aircraft analogy — hence the name 'elevons'. On tail-less aircraft, such as Concorde, elevons are of course the primary means of control.

An analysis of the various forces and moments acting on a hovercraft fitted with elevons is shown in Figure 2. It will be seen that, when the craft makes a turn, *all* the forces acting on the craft, and the moments induced by them, act in a productive manner (indicated by +). Comparison with Figure 1 shows how, on a craft fitted with a conventional vertically-hinged rudder, *all* the forces and moment induced by the rudder (apart from the rudder turning moment itself) are of a counter-productive nature (indicated by —).

Further benefits of elevons

Having devised a promising means of banking the craft by using the differential action of the elevons, and having provided for pitch control from their simultaneous action, a further possibility became apparent: that of thrust control. By providing the elevons with hinge lines close to their centres of pressure it would be possible to move them through large angles with relatively small control forces, until, with the elevons vertical, the rearward flow of air would be completely obstructed. Simultaneous operation of the elevons would thus provide equal control of thrust on both sides. Differential operation would give differential thrust, with the possibility of obtaining full thrust on one side and zero thrust on the other. This would provide a valuable aid to low-speed manoeuvring.

A further very considerable bonus from the control system as then envisaged was its natural adaptability for use on a hovercraft having a single engine to power both lift and propulsion systems. The Missionnaire uses separate engines to allow each system to be operated independently of the other, with a consequent increase in complexity, weight and expense. To adapt the Missionnaire to take advantage of all that this new elevon system of control had to offer would involve a very major modification. Thus a completely new design of craft was evolved, which eventually took shape as the River Rover.

Initial trials with the River Rover prototype soon convinced us of the value of the elevons in improving

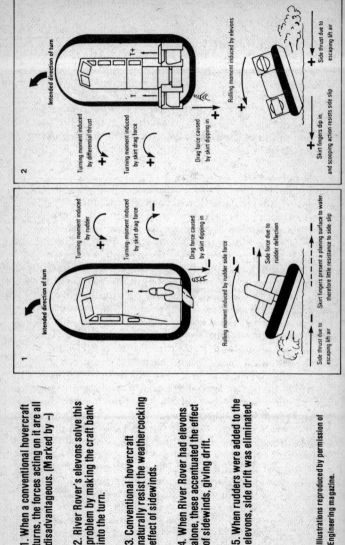

1. When a conventional hovercraft turns, the forces acting on it are all disadvantageous. (Marked by −)

2. River Rover's elevons solve this problem by making the craft bank into the turn.

3. Conventional hovercraft naturally resist the weathercocking effect of sidewinds.

4. When River Rover had elevons alone, these accentuated the effect of sidewinds, giving drift.

5. When rudders were added to the elevons, side drift was eliminated.

Illustrations reproduced by permission of Engineering magazine.

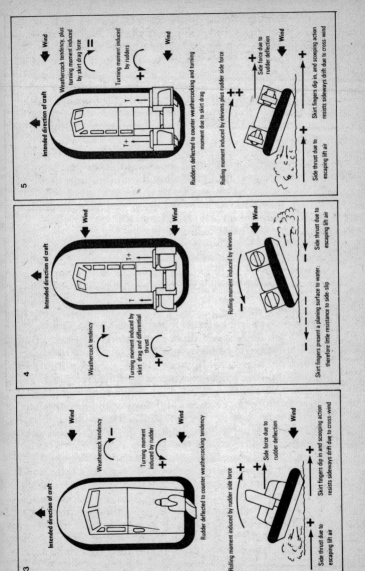

controllability. Under no-wind conditions, banked turns with greatly reduced sideways drift could be executed. However, this required a better understanding of the forces involved before we were able to guarantee a 'good' turn under all conditions.

A relationship between craft forward speed and radius of turn had to be established, such that the positive rolling moment due to elevon action was always greater than the negative moment caused by centrifugal force acting on the craft.

In practice this involved a trial-and-error approach, with the primary object of achieving the smallest possible radius of turn without allowing the craft to slow down below the hump speed. The issue was complicated by several variables, such as the loaded weight of the craft, wind speed and direction, and sea state, but a reliable technique was eventually evolved.

A further benefit is that the elevon concept is not restricted to small hovercraft, and the placing of the pivot at the centre of pressure means that the control forces remain relatively small, even on a large craft.

Effect of wind

It was providential that early tests were carried out on days when there was little or no wind. At this stage of development, no rudders were fitted, nor were they considered necessary. However, when the River Rover was operated under windy conditions for the first time, it nearly ended in disaster. Had we at that time made the analysis shown in Figures 3 and 4 we would have realized what was happening. We would also have realized why, contrary to expectations, the River Rover's predecessor, the Missionnaire, always handled remarkably well under cross-wind conditions. The large fin and rudder would suggest an excessive tendency to 'weathercock' into wind, but in practice it was not difficult to oppose this tendency by using opposite rudder. Examination of Figures 3 and 4 will indicate that, under crosswind conditions, the effects of vertical rudders and horizontal elevons have in fact been reversed. The rolling moment induced by the rudder in keeping the craft on a straight heading now has a beneficial effect, whereas elevons have an adverse effect.

On the River Rover, the problem was solved by the addition of vertical rudders. Elevons could now be used to bank the craft against the wind, and the tendency to turn into wind, due to the combined effects of skirt drag and weathercocking, could be resisted by applying opposite rudder. This opposite rudder has itself a favourable effect in helping to bank the craft against the wind. Thus a method was evolved whereby the craft is banked to windward, and opposite rudder applied to keep straight (Figure 5). This technique is well known to aircraft pilots, who use it to keep lined up on a runway while on the approach for a crosswind landing. On the River Rover, sideways drifting due to crosswinds is substantially reduced, with a consequent marked reduction in drift angle. The benefit is particularly appreciated when approaching a slipway under strong crosswind conditions.

Ultimate proof of the value of this combination of elevons and rudders was provided by the members of the 1978-79 Joint Services Hovercraft Expedition to Nepal. The two River Rovers between them completed some 280 hours of operation in demanding and often dangerous conditions on the Kali Gandaki. Furthermore, the expedition proved that River Rover does not need a trained expert to drive it: all but three of the twenty-six man expedition team had never driven a hovercraft before, yet they all learned to drive the River Rover, with an inhospitable Himalayan river as their only training ground.

A pilot's verdict
Peter Dixon (Captain on Hercules transport aircraft)

The River Rover hovercraft has demonstrated its ability to operate regularly and safely in both directions over a length of the Kali Gandaki measuring sixty-two miles (124-mile round trip). We have driven it routinely over obstacles which could only be attempted by a conventional boat or even by any other hovercraft of comparable or greater carrying capacity, at considerable risk. The craft has an extremely reliable engine — an essential characteristic since there is only one. We have also taken the craft up and down numerous hazardous rapids without major catastrophe. The positive lateral controllability provided by the elevons gives the craft a major advantage in these circumstances.

The major advantage of a hovercraft over other vessels — its ability to operate on land and shallows as well as in deep water — is counterbalanced by its lack of friction with the surface which makes accurate directional control and tight turning difficult. The River Rover's elevon control system reduces this disadvantageous effect to a minimum.

By virtue of its development and construction in a small garage workshop as opposed to a sophisticated factory, and its reliance on a simple bolt-together construction, the River Rover still has room for alterations to ease maintenance. Areas where improvement would be particularly beneficial are the facilities for routine oil changes, the method of adjusting belt tension and the general accessibility of components in the engine/transmission bay.

We had two River Rovers in Nepal and there are a few minor differences between them. One notable example is the experimental fuel system which was fitted to River Rover 02. We found this to be no improvement on the system in Rover 01, which has a conventional inboard tank with outboard long-range takes used to refill the main tank where necessary. Use of Rover 02's system of parallel-feeding outboard tanks can lead to engine stoppage, albeit with a degree of misuse by the driver. Since river operation requires frequent acceleration through hump speed, our experience led us to suggest that the total disposable load should be reduced by 100 pounds from the quoted 1100 pounds for these conditions.

In general, with the exception of the early transmission problems, the River Rover operated very effectively on the swirls and eddies of this testing river. The hull and skirt stood up well to wear and damage, and the engine proved extremely reliable. As an example of River Rover's journey time, the twenty-six miles between Base Camp and Camp 2 typically took one hour twenty minutes, the fastest time being fifty-five minutes with a light load; this is a two-day journey on foot. A difference of this order makes the hovercraft a feasible means of transport in remote areas of developing countries where roads do not exist.

Before the start of the expedition it had been suggested that the River Rover could be driven by, for example, a doctor, in much the same way as a western doctor drives his car when making house calls. Although anyone with reasonable aptitude can be trained to drive the River Rover well in little more time than it takes to learn to drive a car, driving this craft requires considerable concentration. The consequent fatigue might be sufficient to impair the doctor's performance in his primary task. In order for the hovercraft to be used most efficiently in the Fourth World, the ideal arrangement would therefore be a specialized driver/maintenance engineer providing a service to the medical personnel or relief agency which were to use it.

Some misconceptions answered
Ed Chase

River Rover is too sophisticated for the Third World
It is, in fact, very *meccano*-like in construction and is
simpler than a car in its overall design concept. It is *much*
simpler than aircraft which are already used in most of
these countries by organizations such as MAF. It can be
driven by virtually anyone, unlike an aircraft. Attempts
are still being made to simplify the River Rover design
even further.

River Rover is too expensive to buy
Compared with a car it is more expensive, but it is
significantly cheaper than a Cessna aeroplane or fast boat.
(It should never be used if a car or Land Rover could do the
job instead.)

River Rover is too expensive to run
This is not true at all when compared with a boat, which
uses much more fuel for the same speed and payload. We
operated River Rover for $10 per hour, fuel included; to
hire the Alouette helicopter for the BBC filming cost $375
per hour!

River Rover is not capable of getting up rapids
This impression was overemphasized due to the editing
done on the BBC film. River Rover 'Mark III' will have
significantly more thrust and will not suffer the same
blade-shattering problems. And in fact on the Kali
Gandaki, River Rover was regularly tackling rapids which
would be classed as very severe by a canoeist.

River Rover needs too much back-up
The expedition needed a lot of back-up, partly because
River Rover was a new design. But experience in Irian Jaya
shows conclusively that someone with a reasonable
aptitude for car maintenance and a supply of fuel can run a
River Rover anywhere that is not too rough.

Medical report
Robin Dugdale

We were awoken at dawn each morning by the sound of
voices and the inevitable accompaniment of much
coughing and spitting. People would sit patiently waiting
to be seen and often an audience of onlookers and relatives
would gather in the background to gaze in amazement and
laugh at our strange antics. The overwhelming curiosity of
the people was something we had not been prepared for
and it took a lot of getting used to. Every single movement
that we made was studied and discussed. We were
watched wherever we went. There was no hostility; the
villagers were unfailingly friendly towards us but their
unending stares at times could be unnerving.

It was fascinating and also disturbing to be in a country
in which the attitudes and priorities with regard to health
care are so different from our own. There was virtually no
medical care in the villages. Unless there was a
government-sponsored health post nearby, the only local
forms of medicine were the spells and witchcraft of the
holy man of the village. Even where Western medicine
was available, local taboos and prejudices would often
mean that the facilities available would not be used.

In a country where as many as four out of every ten
children fail to reach the age of five years, attitudes to life
and death are bewilderingly different from ours. We saw
many poor little children at our clinic in the most
advanced stages of neglect and malnutrition. Many of them
were brought with chronic ear infections, or neglected
sores and wounds which had become horribly infected. In
most cases we could do no more than apply simple
dressings and attempt to combat the infection with
antibiotics. Many of the children were from large families
and we knew that without our help the family would not
have the resources to support the child who would have to
be allowed to die. I often felt very helpless and depressed

when faced with problems like these.

Many of the things that we saw would have been trivial complaints in the West, but when totally neglected or incorrectly treated, a simple skin wound can soon become a life-threatening condition. We reluctantly had to turn many patients away without even attempting treatment. Others came along just to enjoy the show and see what free medicines and tablets they could get out of us. With our limited resources we therefore had to develop a strict discrimination over who did or did not need treatment and many would-be patients we sent away empty-handed.

Many patients complained of long-standing toothache and the general state of dental care was appalling. We often saw whole mouths of rotting teeth and except for the young, many people had only one or two teeth left. Dental extractions therefore became a regular part of the work of the morning clinic and our expertise in this field rapidly increased. At least it was one form of treatment which was guaranteed to yield dramatic positive results and the patient was invariably delighted when we had successfully removed his painful tooth.

During the early days at the camp, we made contact with the doctors at Tansen Mission Hospital. Despite extreme limitations of finance and endless difficulties in obtaining supplies and equipment, the standard of medicine practised there was of an enviably high standard. The dedication of the staff was an inspiration and we learned much about medicine in Nepal from them. The hospital itself was a simple brick building standing above the town of Tansen along a winding dusty track. The wards were small and crowded. Patients were often in beds in the corridors. Inside the cool and rather dark wards there was constant bustle of activity. The patients would arrive at all times of the day, usually carried on the backs of friends and relatives. We saw patients who had walked for as many as fifteen days to get to the hospital.

Outside the hospital entrance, a little village of thatched mud huts had grown up in order to provide overnight accommodation and food for weary travellers who had crossed Nepal's daunting hills in order to reach the mission hospital. Even so we learned that a woman living within a quarter of a mile of the hospital had recently died because of reluctance to seek help. There is still deep suspicion of Western medicine and often great reluctance to come for treatment. There was a young girl who had crushed her finger in a rice mill. The pain must have been agonizing — but she had waited seven days before coming to hospital. In some cases, the struggle for existence is so grim that medical attention is a luxury which cannot be afforded.

A lot of effort at Tansen is now going into aid of a long-term practical and beneficial nature. There is an extensive programme in co-ordination with the Nepal government to train student nurses, midwives and other paramedical workers so that they can go out into the villages and provide small health posts in rural areas. These posts have the advantage of close contact with the local community: aid can be given where it is really needed, in response to the demands and requirements of the particular villages concerned. However, the inhospitable terrain makes travel between the health posts and the base hospital a laborious and time-consuming matter, and it is in the context of improving medical facilities at a simple village level that the potential of river communications lies. A hovercraft could also be very valuable in any large-scale vaccination programmes or surveys in which it was necessary to contact a large number of people. Certainly the potentialities of the River Rover hovercraft were viewed with enthusiasm by the Tansen staff.

I learned several important lessons during my time in Nepal. Firstly, it gave me a whole new outlook on the sort of Westernized medicine that we practise in Britain. It made me far more appreciative of the facilities which we have and very often take for granted. Secondly, it made me realize that our sophisticated Western medicine is not always the best: in poor developing countries such as Nepal the requirements may be very different. In Nepal, the priorities are still the provision of safe drinking water and the prevention of malnutrition by improved agriculture. Much basic health education is still needed in many remote rural areas. Tuberculosis and leprosy, both of which are diseases of poverty and overcrowding, are still commonplace in Nepal. Only by improving the living standards of the population will these diseases be eradicated.

Thirdly I was very struck by the gulf of culture which lay between Nepal and the West. Western standards and values cannot be imposed upon their society. In the larger cities of Nepal, change is occurring very rapidly and this could have serious consequences for the future stability of the country. The same applies to changes in medicine. Old ideas and beliefs can only be changed gradually by a process of education at a basic village level and by being able to prove that new ideas and methods really do work in practice. Fourthly, I was greatly impressed by the fortitude and courage of a people constantly struggling against a hostile terrain and climate.

From a medical point of view the expedition was a tremendous eye-opener for me. And I was thrilled that we were able to demonstrate that River Rover could be used to improve communications, and thereby health care in needy countries such as Nepal.

Appendix F

Reflections on Nepal
Brian Holdsworth

Nepal is scenically one of the most beautiful countries in
the world. The physical and climatic contrasts between the
low Terai plain in the south, the Mahabharat range of hills
(mountains in any other land), the Kathmandu Valley (a
valley at 4,000 feet) and the mighty Himalayas are
fascinating. All this is compressed into an area of only
75,000 square miles, dissected by great rivers which are
born high up in the perpetual snows, grow to raging
torrents, widen and eventually flow out rather lazily into
India.

Nepal is very poorly endowed with natural resources.
Economically, it is one of the poorest nations in the world.
Disease is rife and the child mortality rate is very high, due
to meagre medical facilities and appalling standards of
hygiene. The people accept their lot philosophically largely
because of their religious beliefs: most are Hindus, some
Buddhists. In Nepal these two religions are curiously
interwoven.

The Nepalese nation derives from a number of regional
tribes and the people still, to a certain degree, belong to
tribes. The people vary considerably in character and
attitudes largely according to the physical diversities of the
land. The hardiest, poorest, most interesting and probably
most likeable are the rather shy people who dwell in the
mountains. The main occupation by far is subsistence
agriculture. For a family, ownership of some land,
preferably good fertile land, is important. The staple diet is
rice and this is the main crop in the lower, well-populated
regions; however I was surprised to see so many fields and
terraced hillsides growing potatoes, maize, wheat and
barley.

One of the biggest and most obvious of Nepal's many
problems is communications. Another less obvious one is
energy. Although the potential for hydro-electric power is

almost infinite, as yet few generating plants exist because of the high capital cost of engineering. Nepal receives considerable injections of foreign aid but much more is needed. Most of the electric power in the big towns and cities is oil-generated. When OPEC raise their oil prices, we in the affluent and greedy West feel aggrieved; such price rises cause *real* hardship to Third and Fourth World countries and stifle their development. Away from the big towns there is no electricity . . . or gas or coal, piped water or sanitation! Wood is burned for cooking, and for warmth if needed; candles provide artificial light; some paraffin or kerosene is used too, but any oil product is expensive. Petrol is expensive, partly due to a hefty tax. The government's options for raising revenue are very few, so most imported goods and commodities are heavily taxed.

I found Nepal's architecture interesting and sometimes quite superb. In the Kathmandu Valley and most towns, building is in brick with tiled roofs. In rural areas most dwellings are of mud construction and thatch; stone and heavy slate predominates in the mountains. There is a spectacular profusion of splendid old pagodas, temples and palaces in the Kathmandu Valley. The exotic shapes, the colours, and absolutely magnificent wood carving exceeded my expectations. A good deal of money — much of it from abroad — and effort is being expended on preserving the best of these national treasures. This fine architecture, together with the massive mountains and the mystique of a remote eastern kingdom, attracts many visitors from Europe, America, Australia and Japan. Tourism is in a sense Nepal's main industry and, apart from foreign aid, its only source of foreign exchange.

It is difficult to express adequately my admiration for the work of the expatriate Christian missions. I was privileged and humbled to spend a day or two enjoying hospitality and fellowship at the mission hospitals and to see the immensity of the task. Most of the tangible front-line effort is in the medical field, but much excellent work is also being done with industrial training and in other areas of education and development. Christian doctors, nurses and administrators of various nationalities, most of whom have given up highly-paid appointments in their

own countries, are here working for a pittance,
performing miracles with basic equipment in sometimes
ramshackle buildings. The missionaries can only preach by
example as it is a legal offence to attempt to persuade a
person to change his religion. Nevertheless, there is
already a singificant number of Nepalese Christians.

Nepal is governed by King Birenda — a virtually
absolute, but benign, monarch (educated at Eton College)
— and his council of ministers. There are various grades of
administration with officials and councils appointed right
down to village level. This is the *Panchayat* system. It has
disadvantages, including what we regard as corruption,
but seems to work adequately. I believe that the King is
entirely dedicated to furthering the best interests of his
people. He has seen chaos and suffering result from too
rapid a pace of change in other Third World states and
believes Nepal can only cope with gradual progress.

Having visited Nepal, I would tend to agree. I trust that
painful revolution can be avoided and that progress
towards improving the quality of life for many millions of
Nepalis will be rational, steady and appropriate to the
country's needs.

Appendix G

Team members

Pilot Officer Hugh Bennell, RAF (19 years)
Skima pilot, trek reporter

Corporal Ben Bennett, REME (27 years)
Engineer, advance party

Captain Gerry Bradnam, Royal Corps of Transport (46 years)
Deputy Leader, chief hovercraft pilot

Surgeon Lieutenant Donald Bruce, RN (25 years)
Medical officer, part-time dentist, riverside creative chef, ornithologist

Tony Burgess (40 years)
Hovercraft designer and engineer

Ed Chase (27 years)
Engineer, technical reporter, hand-over of Rover 02 in Irian Jaya

Squadron Leader Michael Cole, RAF (45 years)
Expedition leader

Bernard Coleman (33 years)
TEAR Fund engineer, hand-over of Rover 02 in Irian Jaya

Petty Officer Doug Cooledge, RN (38 years)
Engineer, electrician, Channel crossing

Major Dennis Cooper, Royal Army Education Corps (54 years)
Advance party leader, road transport, interpreter

Flight Lieutenant Peter Dixon, RAF (29 years)
Hovercraft driver, technical reporter

Squadron Leader Robin Dugdale, RAF (30 years)
Medical Officer, part-time dentist, excellent field-kitchen baker

Sergeant Rick Elliott, REME (29 years)
Engineer, field workshop, first aid, fuel specialist

Captain Neil Fisher, Queen's Gurkha Signals (26 years)
Advance party, signals, trek leader

Corporal Stuart Forbes, RAF (24 years)
Engineer, Gemini pilot, mountaineer

Flight Lieutenant Paddy Gallacher, RAF (34 years)
Logistics, air movements, surf sail experimenter

Sergeant Brian Goodwin, RAF (42 years)
Photographer, volunteer assistant at clinics

Lieutenant Commander Brian
Holdsworth, RN (49 years)
*Rear party leader, officer i/c Base
Camp*

Tim Longley (46 years)
River Rover designer

Corporal Tony Maher, Royal
Marines (24 years)
*Gemini coxswain, first aid,
'conjurer-up' of items for
expedition, riverside entertainer*

Staff Sergeant David Porter,
Royal Engineers (36 years)
Surveyor, riverside artist

Corporal Purnasing Gurung,
1/2nd King Edward VII's Own
Gurkha Rifles (29 years)
Interpreter, Nepali liaison

Corporal Mick Reynolds, REME
(24 years)
*Engineer, Skima pilot, Channel
crossing*

Lieutenant John Rollins, Royal
Signals (24 years)
Signals, i/c canoeing, trek leader

Lance Corporal Shovaram Bura,
1/2nd King Edward VII's Own
Gurkha Rifles (26 years)
*Interpreter, Nepali liaison, i/c
stores*

Chief Technician Bruce Vincent,
RAF (42 years)
Chief engineer, mountaineer

The Hovering Doctor Service, Irian Jaya

Les Henson (41 years)
*A trained mechanical engineer, working for the British National
Coal Board for seven years. In 1977 joined RBMU with his Dutch
wife Wapke and began work at Sumo in the heart of Irian Jaya.
Their son Joel, born there. First operator of Hovering Doctor Service.*

David Henderson (45 years)
*Ten years service in the Royal Navy. In 1968 joined FEBA radio
project in the Seychelles as civil engineer and radio producer. In
1973 became RBMU Extension Secretary.*

BBC TV World About Us team

Tony Salmon   Producer
Jenny Cropper   Assistant Producer
Ian Stone   Senior Cameraman
John Beck   Cameraman
Mervyn Broadway   Sound Recordist

Expedition helpers from the Sherpa Co-operative Trekking

Santo Bir Lama	Sirdar
Rambahadur Lama	Cook
Sitiman Lama	Cook's assistant
Kembahadur Lama	Porter
Kusang Lama	Porter
Ramansigh	Minibus driver
Hari-Chhetri	Driver's assistant

Appendix H

General acknowledgements

The expedition gratefully acknowledges the help and support of the following organizations and individuals.

Joint Services Expedition Trust
Renault UK (major sponsor)
J. Swire and Sons (Hong Kong)
Overseas development Administration (ODA)
Joint Services Medical Supply Depot
MOD Supplies and Transport (Royal Navy)
Royal Navy Hovercraft Trials Unit, Lee-on-Solent
Royal Navy Aircraft Yard, Fleetlands
Gurkha Movements Detachment, Kathmandu
Royal Navy Victuallers, Botley
RAF Air Movements
RAF Airport Unit Kai Tak
British Embassy, Kathmandu
BBC TV-World About Us
National Exhibition Centre, Birmingham
BMMF International
Missionary Aviation Fellowship (UK and USA)
Regions Beyond Missionary Union
Shining Hospital, Pokhara
TEAR Fund
UMN Hospital, Tansen
UMN Butwal Technical Institute
Gorsley Baptist Church

Sherpa Co-operative Trekking, Kathmandu
Save the Children Fund, Kathmandu
Seaspeed
Williams and Glyn's Bank, Farnborough
MRAF Sir Neil Cameron, GCB CBE DSO DFC AE
Sir Maurice Laing
Captain J. H. Beadon, RN
Group Captain P. J. Shelley, MBE RAF
Lt Col J. Cross OBE 7GR
Wg Cdr S. D. Baldock, MBE DFM RAF
Lt Cdr E. Palmer, RN
Major R. L. J. Pott, MC MBE
Major R. Tregarthen, RAOC
Sqn Ldr R. L. B. Bell, RAF
Sqn Ldr W. B. Underwood, MBE RAF
Capt (QGO) Dhandhoj Tamang
Flight Lieutenant A. Cutler, RAF
Flying Officer R. Abbott, RAF
Fleet Chief A. Lockwood, RN
Mr Brian Bennell
Mr Duncan Bluck
Mr Denis Collins
Mr Alan Dakers
Mr John Douglas
Mr Tom Frank
Rev. Pat Goodland, MBE

Mr I. B. Gurung
Dr Bill Gould
Mr Peter Hitchin
Mr Mike Ive
Mr Ken Johnston
Mr John Kembery
Mr Krishnadass Rai
Mr Geoff Larcombe
Dr Dick Matern
Mr Eric Mantell
Mr Jeffrey Mee
Dr Graham Morris

Mr Len Paige
Mr Arthur Pont
Mr Michael Pinder
Mr Michael Pinkess
Mr Colin Reilly
Mr Brian Russell
Dr Denis Roche
Mr Lee Seaman
Mr Paul Spivey
Mr Bob Skelton
Mr David Stavely

Finance

Finance for the expedition was generously provided by the following.

Renault UK
Overseas Development
  Administration (ODA)
Joint Services Expedition
  Trust
Royal Navy, Army and RAF
  Expedition Training Funds
J. Swire and Sons (Hong Kong)
BP Oil Ltd
Douglas Civil Engineers
J. Lucas Industries Ltd
Bostrom UOP Ltd
Kwikstik Ltd
Royal Navy Sailors' Fund
Dairy Farm (Hong Kong)

H. Kadoorie CBE (Hong Kong)
Royal Geographical Society
Mount Everest Foundation
Norcros Ltd
ICI Plastics Ltd
Canbury (Smithfield) Ltd
St Luke's Chapel RAF
  Hospital, Ely
Grantown-on-Spey Baptist
  Church
Service Associations, Ships and
  Units of the team members
Personal contributions of
  team members

Equipment and services donated to expedition

The following companies generously donated equipment and services.

Renault UK (two engines and spares)

Alcan (aluminium extrusions and sheeting)

Northern Rubber (rubber for hovercraft skirts)

BP Oils Ltd (oils)

J. Lucas (solar panels, batteries, cable, electrical parts)

John Swire and Sons, Hong Kong:
China Navigation Ship Company (freight space)
Cathay Pacific Airways (airline tickets)

Bostrom Division UOP Ltd (seats for hovercraft)

Kwikstik Products Ltd (Kwikseal tape)

Davall Gears (steel pulleys)

Maclellan Rubbers (fendering)

Triplex Windscreens (windscreens)

International Yacht Paints (paints and compounds)

Smith Vehicle Instruments (panel instruments)

BRD Aldridge (flexible drive couplings)

Goodyear Tyre Company (drive fan belts)

ICI Plastics (perspex panels)

RHP Transmission Bearings (bearings)

C. T. Bowrings & Co Ltd (high-risk insurance at reduced premium)

Chubb Fire (fire extinguishers)

Trico Ltd (windscreen wipers and washers)

Pye (radio for Channel crossing)

Filpour (water filtration equipment)

RFD Inflatables Ltd (loan of life rafts)

British Oxygen Company (portable welding kit)

T. W. Beech (packaged food)

OMC Johnsons (fuel tanks)

Baracuda (wind surfer)

Rolex Ltd (loan of watch)

Ingersoll (watches for engineers)

The London Fan Company (hovercraft fan blades)

Erskine System Ltd (generator)

Newton Chambers Ltd (water pump)

Heron Optical (monocular glasses)

Burton McCall (sweaters)

Polaroid (sunglasses)

Callard & Bowser, and Nuttall (sweets for Nepali children)

Clarks (trekking boots)

Tufnol (Tufnol block)

Skil Tools GB (loan of field workshop tools)

Coopers Gaskets (engine gaskets)

Dolby Brothers (accounts book)

Kangol (seat safety belts)

Miltech (ranger systems)

Rainbow Video (video tape)

National Panasonic (cassette tape recorder)

Caswell & Co (boot dubbin)

Services Kinema Corporation SKC (film)

Hasselblad, and Leeds Camera (loan of cameras)

Kodak Ltd (film)

DJM Records (recording cassettes)

Bibliography

R. and L. Fleming, *Kathmandu Valley*, Kodansha.

Jonathan Lindell, *Nepal and the Gospel of God*, United Mission of Nepal, Kathmandu.

Michel Peissel, *The Great Himalayan Passage*, Collins.

Francis Tuker, *Gorkha*, Constable & Co.